YESTERDAY'S WHITEFRIARS

Historic photo-odyssey reveals a rich tapestry of Canterbury life

YESTERDAY'S WHITEFRIARS

*Historic photo-odyssey reveals a rich
tapestry of Canterbury life*

COMPILED BY
PAUL CRAMPTON

Kent Messenger
Group Newspapers

breedon **books**
PUBLISHING

First published in Great Britain in 2002 by
The Breedon Books Publishing Company Limited
Breedon House, 3 The Parker Centre,
Derby, DE21 4SZ.

ISBN 1 85983 298 9

Printed and bound by Butler & Tanner, Frome,
Somerset, England.

Jackets printed by Lawrence-Allen, Avon, England

Contents

Introduction

MEDIAEVAL Canterbury could be divided into quadrants, each dominated by a large monastic complex set within sizeable walled precincts. The north-east quadrant was dominated by the Cathedral and Christ Church Priory, a Benedictine order, very much as the Cathedral and King's School do today. The north-west and south-east sections were dominated by the Benedictine Blackfriars and the Franciscan Greyfriars respectively.

The south-east quadrant contained the church, associated buildings and walled precinct of the Augustinian Whitefriars, established in 1324 and dissolved in 1538. After centuries as a private house in substantial grounds, the Whitefriars site was used to construct the Simon Langton Boys' and Girls' Schools, opened in 1881. Both schools were gradually expanded over the following 50 years. Beyond the school grounds, in those pre-war years, the rest of the quadrant was covered by tiny lanes crowded with ancient buildings. The exception was the grand late Georgian and Regency houses of St George's Terrace, which were part of the early 19th-century expansion of the south-east suburbs of the city. Our area also included two churches, namely the Church of England St Mary Bredin in Rose Lane and the Countess of Huntingdon's Connexion Congregational Church in Watling Street.

The infamous Baedeker raid of 1 June 1942 was concentrated on the south-east quadrant of the city and the Whitefriars area in particular. No other part of the city was nearly so badly affected. The immediate post-blitz demolition and clearance policy was equally as uncompromising. Both churches mentioned above were gutted by incendiary bombs, but capable of repair. However, St Mary Bredin Church had been demolished by the autumn of that year. The shell of the Congregational Church remained but, ironically, was destroyed in the daylight raid of 31 October 1942. Other properties in Watling Street and Rose Lane perished at the same time. When the dust settled, only around 30 per cent of the pre-war buildings, in the Whitefriars area, were left standing.

As recently as the late 1940s, there were still significant remains of the mediaeval Whitefriars friary remaining above ground, including fragments of the church and lengths of the original precincts wall. These relics would disappear as the post-war redevelopment of the area gathered pace. However, before the buildings of the brave new Whitefriars could appear, much of the area was used to stage the Canterbury Festival Exhibition of 1951. The exhibition commemorated the city's numerous involvements between church and state, as well as giving the citizens a chance to see the plans for the rebuilding of the blitzed areas.

The 1950s saw the redevelopment of the south side of St George's Street, dominated by the new colonnaded terrace of shops. David Nixon opened a new store for Barretts in 1954, on a prestigious corner plot between St George's Street and a widened Rose Lane. In 1956, the bus station relocated to a new purpose built site in St George's Lane and during the following year, a new Sun Building rose from the site of its blitzed predecessor. The new Congregational Church was finally finished in 1958, after a protracted construction period fraught with problems. All of these new 1950s buildings respected the scale of a mediaeval city and therefore, rested easily alongside their older neighbours, despite the modernist architectural styles used.

In the 1960s, redevelopment of the Whitefriars area went into overdrive. The vast majority of the old buildings that had survived the blitz were pulled down from 1960 to 1965. In the same period, all the once tiny lanes were considerably widened. The scale of the new buildings put up in this decade was now much larger and their styles more overtly modernist (or even Brutalist, in the case of the multi-storey car park). A massive new department store for Riceman's opened with much ceremony in 1962. Unfortunately, six months after its elaborate opening, the store caught fire. Luckily, the damage was concentrated in the rooftop Grace & Favour restaurant. David

Jacobs performed the official re-opening ceremony in September 1963.

1968 marked the beginning of the construction for the aforementioned multi-storey car park that was opened the following year by Lord Buchanan. Probably the most controversial building in all of post-war Canterbury, its strong architectural lines, particularly those of the staircase towers, were appreciated by few. The Whitefriars shopping centre was put up in the early 1970s, which also provided an extension for both Marks & Spencer and Riceman's. Finally in 1973, the Morelli's bridge over Gravel Walk linked the new shopping centre with the multi-storey.

Much more was planned for the Whitefriars area than was actually built. A planning concept that dated back to the 1930s was the Civic Centre, destined for the Watling Street car park site. Firm plans and detailed models of it were made in the 1960s, only for the whole scheme to be forcibly scrapped under the threat of local government re-organisation.

The Whitefriars area that existed from the mid-1970s onwards, contained a high percentage of public highway and service areas. This was not helped by the considerable width of Gravel Walk, constructed as the first stage of a cross-city relief road that was never completed. There was also a perceived need for more retail space. Consequently, in 1988, the comprehensive redevelopment of the whole area on a much denser basis was considered. Eventually, four rival development schemes were put out to public consultation and ultimately, a winner chosen. Of the existing buildings in the designated area, the only escapees from the bulldozer would be Marks & Spencer, including its early 1970s extension, part of the colonnaded terrace in St George's Street and, after a last minute change of plan, the former Barrett's store on the St George's Street – Rose Lane corner.

The destruction of modernist Whitefriars began in late 1999, with the demolition of the former Sun Building and adjacent shops in St George's Lane. At the time of writing, the only doomed building still remaining was the Riceman's complex. Peripheral new buildings had been completed, although the centre of the site, including much of the long lost monastic precinct, was still to be redeveloped. It is sad to reflect that of all the mediaeval religious houses mentioned at the beginning of this foreword, only the Whitefriars has been completely obliterated above ground. Moreover, considering the substantial foundations and underground servicing required for the new scheme, it is unlikely that anything of it will remain below ground either. Whitefriars will exist in name only.

Acknowledgements

The vast majority of the pictures reproduced herein come from the archives of the Messenger Group Newspapers, although many of them have never appeared in either the *Kent Messenger* or *Kentish Gazette*. Much of the remainder came from the author's collection, which includes the Fisk Moore archive.

However, a few photographs came from private individuals and other sources, so I would like to thank the following for providing material: Canterbury Museums, Clive Bowley, Edward Wilmot, Derek Butler, Anthony Swaine, John Martin, David Riceman, Rob Williams, Stan Kemp, Barrett's, Tony Huggett and Canterbury Archaeological Trust.

The feature 'Canterbury Then and Now' by Paul Crampton, appears regularly in the *Kentish Gazette*.

Before the Blitz

PRE-WAR Whitefriars was not that much different from the rest of Canterbury, a sleepy market town crowded with tiny lanes, ill suited to the age of the motor vehicle. The exception was the walled precinct and buildings of the Simon Langton Schools, which will be discussed in their own chapter.

The area contained two churches, an oast house, a large brewery complex and an elegant terrace of late Georgian and Regency houses that swept up and along the old city wall ramparts. There was also a 16th-century house, the subject of many postcard views, that was reputed to be the birthplace of playwright Christopher Marlowe. It could be found on the eastern corner between St George's Street and St George's Lane.

Many people also lived in the Whitefriars area before the blitz. There were cottages on the east side of St George's Lane opposite the Simon Langton School and terraced houses on both sides of Watling Street. Further dwellings could be found in Rose Lane, including a rectangle of humble cottages behind Marks & Spencer called Rose Square. Finally, to go up market, the south side of Gravel Walk boasted two fine detached houses.

By the beginning of the 1930s, modernisation of the area was being considered. St George's Street was the most prestigious part of Canterbury's main thoroughfare and its south side falls within our study area. Here, Marks & Spencer demolished three old properties and built a new store, which opened in 1930. A rear extension into Rose Square was added in 1939. In the mid-1930s, Woolworth's built a new shop on the same side of the main street and nearly opposite St George's Church. Another new shop building was also planned and this would have replaced the ancient Pollard's Jeweller, had World War Two not intervened.

Canterbury City Council also had modernisation in mind for the Whitefriars area. They conceived the idea of a Civic Centre just off the Dane John, to be linked to the Cathedral by a Civic Way. In the mid-1930s, the redundant Dane John Brewery was demolished in preparation. Please see the chapter on Whitefriars Unrealised for more details.

The Riding Gate, one of the main entrances to the Whitefriars area, seen here in the early 1880s. The late 18th-century brick arch would give way to a wrought iron bridge in 1883.

The early 19th-century Regency terrace off the Dane John in 1941. Note the uncut grass. The furthest house in the row (no. 1) would perish in the October 1942 blitz.

Taken from a Dane John property, this 1930s view captures not only the roofs of the terraced houses in Watling Street, but also the Congregational and St Mary Bredin Churches.

The solid Victorian Dane John Brewery, on the corner of Watling Street and Marlowe Avenue, at the turn of the last century. Citing poor water quality as the reason, the brewery relocated to Hythe in about 1930.

The rear of the brewery in the yard accessed from Marlowe Avenue (left). The entire complex would be demolished in the mid-1930s.

Mr Frederick George Crampton, the author's great-grandfather and former employee of Dane John Brewery, with the author's grandfather and father in about 1934.

The top section of Rose Lane, seen from its junction with Watling Street, in the late 19th century. The picture is dominated by the then recently built St Mary Bredin Church.

The humble late 18th-century cottages of Rose Square in 1930, situated just off Rose Lane, near the St George's Street end. The building work (left) is for a narrow rear entrance to the new Marks & Spencer store, opened the same year.

An impression of nos 30 to 36 St George's Street in about 1940. No. 31 is part of The Parade Chambers and nos 34 to 36: Marks & Spencer.

Nos 37 to 47, no. 39 being the offices of the *Kentish Gazette*, no. 43: Castle & Co, wine merchants and no. 46: outfitter Miss E. Martyn.

The final sequence of nos 48 to 56. No. 49 is the *Kentish Observer* office, no. 53: the empty former Pollard's jeweller and 56: the Coach and Horses pub.

Canterbury Silver Band, including the author's grandfather (second row, far right), march past the former Canterbury club (no. 33) and Parade Chambers, in the early 1930s.

The Bakers Temperance Hotel in the 1920s, which would relocate to Ivy Lane in the 1930s. Its old premises would then become the Parade Chambers.

A rare interior shot of the inside of the early 17th-century Bakers Temperance Hotel, this view looking out of the lounge and across into the foyer area.

Pollard's the jeweller in the 1920s, not long after the timbers of the façade had been uncovered. The building was threatened with demolition in the late 1930s, but the plans cancelled by the outbreak of war.

Late afternoon Christmas shopping in St George's Street during the mid-1930s. The brightly lit shop front, far left, is from the recently built Woolworth's store (no. 54).

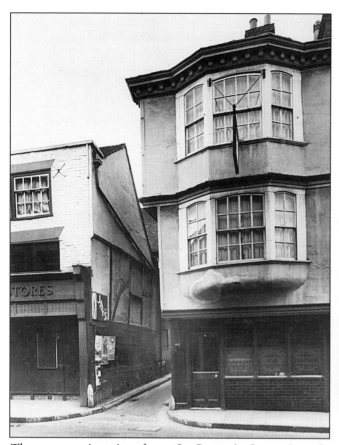

The narrow junction from St George's Street into St George's Lane, in 1941. The Coach & Horses is right, and left, the 16th-century house reputed to be the birth-place of playwright Christopher Marlowe (no. 57).

An earlier view of a tumble-down no. 57, seen from St George's Lane. Unlike the St George's Street elevation, by now hidden behind a late Georgian façade, the rear of the building gave away its true age.

A famous view of Edwardian St George's Street, with many of the buildings on its south side (left) clearly visible. Of interest is the pre-restoration Pollard's façade and the 12 flued chimneystack of the lofty Castle & Co building.

A less well-known view of St George's Street from the beginning of the 20th century, complete with horse-drawn bus heading eastwards.

Hundreds of people crowded into St George's Gate and St George's Street on 29 May 1897, for a visit to the city by the Prince of Wales. The imposing brick building to the left, later part of the Sun Insurance Office, is on the corner up to St George's Terrace.

The tiled roofs and rear elevations of the old, mainly timber-framed buildings, grouped around the St George's Lane – St George's Street junction. Far right is the back of the Marlowe birthplace and to its left, the three-storey Coach and Horses.

Another cityscape, like the one above, taken from the rear of a St George's Terrace property. Below are cottages in St George's Lane. Opposite them are Jenning's print works and left, no. 13 St George's Lane, a house that would still be there in 1960.

The slope up to St George's Terrace from St George's Street, in 1941. The plainer two-storey houses would soon give way to a row of imposing stuccoed Regency style houses of around the 1820s (nos 6 to 12).

The entire three-storey length of St George's Terrace is visible in this 1932 view of an Invicta Motors sponsored Concours D'Elegance in the Cattle Market. The property's domestic offices were accessible from ground level in St George's Lane behind.

The sturdier but plainer two and three-storey houses at nos 13 to 15 St George's Terrace in 1941.

Greek style detailing could be found in nos 16 and 17.

Another view of the Concours D'Elegance, including much of St George's Terrace.

St Mary Bredin Church

THE history of this church has been written many times, so I will merely summarise its early years. Established elsewhere in the early mediaeval period, St Mary Bredin moved to its Rose Lane site and a new church building, in the 13th century.

Largely unchanged for 600 years, the church was subject to a complete rebuild in the 1860s, on the same site. The new much larger church boasted an impressive octagonal tower at its south-east corner, topped by an octagonal spire. Some internal monuments and commemorative tablets were transferred over from the old church building, notably those of the Mann family who once lived in the nearby Jacobean house in Watling Street that survives today. My own family connection to the church is that my father was christened here in October 1932.

St Mary Bredin Church was gutted by fire in the Baedeker raid of 1 June 1942. However, contemporary photographs show the surviving shell to be in good condition and capable of repair. Nevertheless, the demolition gangs soon moved in and the ruins had gone by the autumn of the same year. The desire to demolish rather than repair is not surprising given the ruthless post-blitz clearance policy adopted all over Canterbury. It must also be noted that St Mary Bredin stood in the path of the proposed Civic Way, a grand processional roadway conceived in the early 1930s that would link the Cathedral with the Civic Centre, planned for the former Dane John Brewery site. Moreover, £27,000 was paid out in war damage claims for the 'loss' of the old church. Before long, the congregation moved to a temporary building in Nunnery Fields, near the entrance to Nunnery Fields Hospital.

The last traces of the old St Mary Bredin Church were removed in 1952, to allow for the widening of Rose Lane opposite the Gravel Walk junction. Finally in 1957, the congregation moved further down Nunnery Fields and into a brand new red brick church building. The foundations at the west ends of both mediaeval and Victorian churches were excavated in 1980 prior to the Marlowe Arcade development. Hopefully, the east end of St Mary Bredin, which falls within our study area, will also be examined prior to the current Whitefriars scheme.

The 13th-century church, seen from Gravel Walk, in the early 1860s. It was at this time that a decision to rebuild on the same site was made.

The imposing replacement for the small mediaeval church nears completion in 1868. Only the octagonal spire for the similarly octagonal tower has yet to be added. Note the triple lancet window in the chancel wall, clearly inspired by the earlier church.

The east end of the church in December 1913, looking from the south aisle and over to the font and chancel (right).

Canon Joseph Bambridge looks out of the main south-east door in December 1913.

The author's grandfather, Edward Henry (Harry) Crampton, holds David Edward Crampton, the author's father, at about the time of his christening at St Mary Bredin Church.

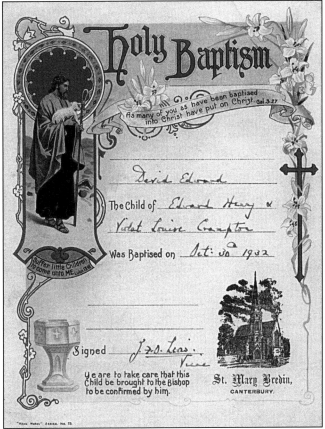

A copy of the author's father's baptismal certificate, dated 30 October 1932.

The familiar octagonal tower and spire of the Victorian church, as seen from the narrow top end of Rose Lane, in the 1930s.

The chancel and altar of St Mary Bredin in the 1930s. The base of the tower, and the main entrance to the church, is to the right.

Smoke still rises from the burnt out ruin of the church, as seen from St Margaret's Street, early in the morning of 1 June 1942.

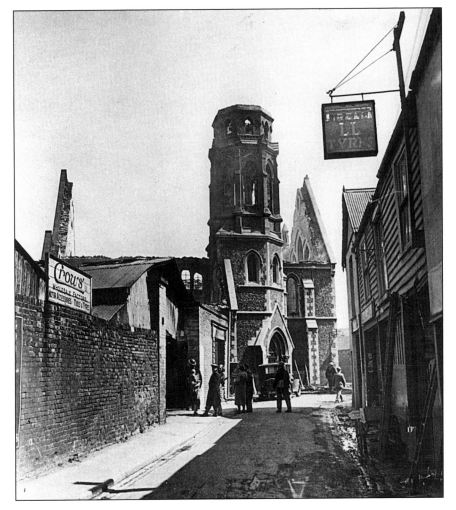

The gutted, yet otherwise intact shell of the church, shortly after the Baedeker raid of 1 June 1942. Note the intact properties in Rose Lane (right). These would perish in the October raid later the same year.

The west end interior of the church, shortly after the incendiary fires had died down. Note the shattered roof tile fragments all over what is left of the floor.

A mural monument to William Mann who died in 1615. It had been relocated from the earlier church. Note the family coat of arms above.

A more damaged tablet to Sir Christopher Mann (died 1638). Presumably, these relics were lost when the gutted church was demolished.

The battered interior, as it was in August 1942, just prior to the levelling of the shell of St Mary Bredin. Another damaged and unidentified mural tablet is visible.

The last visible fragment of St Mary Bredin Church being removed in 1952, prior to the widening of parts of Rose Lane. The man with the pneumatic drill is standing on the remains of a buttress at the south-east corner of the lost church.

The site of the old church, or at least its west end, in 1975.

The new St Mary Bredin Church nears completion, at the bottom of Nunnery Fields, in early 1957.

The foundations of the west ends to both 13th-century and Victorian churches, uncovered in an archaeological dig during June 1980. Because of earlier road widening, the remains at the east end, were now well beneath Rose Lane.

The Sun Buildings

IN THE pre-war years, the Sun Life Assurance Company traded from a charming group of buildings on the corner of St George's Street and St George's Terrace, which also extended up the sloping rampart of the latter. The group was dominated by the corner building, a brick clad former house with tall gables that probably dated from the early Georgian period, but whose façade may have hidden an earlier structure. Another building in the group, on the St George's Terrace slope, sat on a stone vaulted undercroft of early mediaeval date. Moreover in 1906, historian Walter Cozens published a picture of a 'Saxon arch' reputed to be in the cellar of one of the buildings in the Sun group.

The entire Sun Building complex was completely gutted by incendiary bombs on 1 June 1942. The demolition cranes levelled the burnt out structures in the weeks that followed.

Subsequently, Sun Insurance set up in temporary premises at the bottom of Castle Street, an arrangement that was to last for 15 years.

In the meantime, the site of their former office complex was becoming completely overgrown with the ubiquitous Buddleia. The company were not allowed to redevelop their old site as it fell within the area of compulsory purchase, designated by the city council for the rebuilding of the central blitzed area under their complete control. However, by the mid-1950s, the council's plans had been greatly scaled back due to cost. Consequently, a new Sun Building was constructed on the site of the old one, completed and ready for business in December 1957.

The new modernist building was a rectangular structure that backed on to the slope up to St George's Terrace. Here, a landscaped seating area was fashioned. The new Sun Building's main elevation fronted St George's Lane, where a single-storey projection followed the curve of the lane's junction with the main street. In recent years, the building has become more familiar as the offices of the Halifax Building Society and in this guise, it was finally demolished for the Whitefriars development scheme in December 1999 through to January 2000. A realigned St George's Lane now occupies the site.

St George's Gate, with St George's Street beyond, in the 1910s. To the left and at the junction with St George's Terrace, is a large ivy clad 17th-century house with a later brick façade. Then, this was a gentleman's club, complete with smoking & billiard room.

An earlier view from the 1890s, not long after the corner building had been re-clad in red brick and occupied by the East Kent Club.

No. 59 St George's Street in the 1930s, now the premises of the Sun Insurance Office Ltd and with the adjacent buildings in St George's Terrace (left), known collectively as the Sun Buildings. Note the newly inserted corner doorway.

The gentleman's club as it extended up the slope of St George's Terrace. The gabled portion is said to have had an ancient vaulted undercroft beneath it.

The corner Sun Building on 4 June 1942, following severe damage by incendiary bombs and the subsequent demolition of much of its external walls.

The gutted Sun Buildings in St George's Terrace, with their blackened devastated interiors visible and the remnants of ivy still clinging to the façades.

By August 1942, the demolition gangs had passed along St George's Terrace and levelled everything in their wake.

The site of the Sun buildings in early 1952, with their overgrown cellars, and those of adjacent lost buildings, fenced off for safety.

With planning barriers lifted, the foundations for a new Sun Building are sunk on the same site in August 1955. Note the fragments of the former buildings appearing in and around the excavated trenches.

The finishing touches being applied to the new Sun Building in December 1957. Only the landscaping on the St George's Terrace slope (left) remains to be done.

The Sun Building from St George's Terrace on 31 January 1959. The landscaped seating area is now finished and includes telephone boxes relocated from the former cattle market area.

More familiar in recent years as the Halifax Building Society, the former Sun Building being demolished in December 1999. A realigned St George's Lane now occupies much of the site.

The 1940s

THE blitz of Canterbury is probably the most well documented period of the city's recent history. I myself have written several books on the subject. Of all the attacks sustained by the city, the infamous Baedeker raid of the early hours of 1 June 1942 was the most destructive. Enemy scouts had dropped flares on the centre of the city that lit up the Cathedral. Then, at the last minute, a breeze got up and the flares drifted over into the south-east quadrant of the city and its suburbs. This is why that part of the city, and the Whitefriars area in particular, bore the brunt of the attack. Incendiary bombs clattered on to the ancient pitched roofs and burnt away largely unattended.

The National Fire Service rightly prioritised the setting up of fire breaks elsewhere in the city to prevent the fire's spread. High explosive bombs added to the chaos and devastation. Subsequent minor raids in the first week of June added to the destruction and counted the Congregational Church in Watling Street amongst the victims.

The next disaster occurred on the Saturday afternoon of 31 October 1942 when enemy raiders took advantage of the fact that Canterbury's protective bar-rage balloons were grounded for repair. High explosive bomb damage was sustained in small pockets across the city. Whitefriars did not escape, with much damage being inflicted on properties in Rose Lane and Watling Street.

When the dust had settled and the overly thorough post-blitz demolition gangs had swept across the Whitefriars area, only around one third of the pre-war stock of buildings were left standing. Late 1940s demolition accounted for further cottages in Watling Street and St George's Lane.

Much of the mid and late 1940s were taken up with the planning of the new city and the devastated Whitefriars area figured largely in the discussions. The aborted Holden Plan of 1945 (see Whitefriars Unrealised) gave way to the Wilson Plan of 1947 that was to be implemented in 1951. Under Hugh Wilson, who was the City Architect, all of our study area was to be compulsorily purchased by the City Council, so that the development of the area could be co-ordinated between new buildings and the extensive road widening intended for the quadrant. The City Council claimed that this could not be carried out by individual plot owners on a private basis.

The top end of Watling Street, seen beyond a blackened Riding Gate Bridge, in 1946. Nos 1 and 2 Watling Street are on the right, with the white painted side wall of no. 7 visible further down. Reminders of war are still visible all around.

The devastated cottages on the south (Dane John) side of Watling Street, following the daylight raid of 31 October 1942. An embarrassed man had to be rescued from his wrecked bathroom. Nos 38 to 42, seen further down, would survive for now.

The opposite side of the street in the aftermath of the daylight raid. Workmen use a roof timber to push over the remains of the façade to the Countess of Huntingdon Church, brought down by a high explosive bomb. The Dane John Tavern is just visible, right.

The top end of Rose Lane during clear-up operations that followed the October 1942 daylight raid. Philpot's Garage (right) has been devastated. By this time, the shell of St Mary Bredin Church, which would have been visible beyond, had been demolished.

An aerial view of Watling Street, Rose Lane and Gravel Walk in 1947. In the foreground (left), the derelict cottages at nos 38 to 42 Watling Street still remain, as does a single cottage in Watling Square to their right. Philpot's garage is middle left.

The ruins at the bottom end of Rose Lane on 1 June 1942. Left is the tottering façade of the former Fountain Tap pub and right, the rear of the Parade Chambers.

Roughly the same view in the summer of 1946. Passers by watch amateur archaeologists dig in the cellars of the lost Parade Chambers complex.

Dawn on 1 June 1942. Service personnel and firemen crowd St George's Street as the fires on either side are being damped down. Marks & Spencer is far right.

A general view of the bottom end of Rose Lane and the west end of St George's Street, in mid-June 1942. Demolition cranes can be seen at work below centre. The surviving Marks & Spencer can be seen clearly on the left.

Prince George, the Duke of Kent, chats to staff of Marks & Spencer during his visit to the city on 4 June 1942. Some of these women will appear in another photograph in the chapter on the 1960s.

The burnt out interior of the Conservative club, behind the Singer Sewing Machine shop at no. 40 St George's Street, in July 1942. Immediately right, is the print works of the *Kentish Gazette*, which survived the blitz and would remain in use until 1954.

St George's Street, as seen from the roof of Marks & Spencer, in July 1942. Below right is the *Kentish Gazette* print works, their street front office building (no. 39) now a pile of rubble. Further up are the sites of the Singer shop, Bing's and Mac Fisheries.

Activity at the west end of St George's Street towards the end of the decade. The familiar façade of Marks & Spencer stands alone. The bicycle is much in evidence at this time.

A common site in late 1940s St George's Street, the faded painted notices advising passers-by of who once traded here and some-times, where they could be found now. Here, we see the sites of both E. Bing & Son (no. 41) and Mac Fisheries (no. 42).

The middle section of St George's Street the morning after the June 1942 blitz. The three curved arches are all that is left of the *Kentish Observer* (no. 49) and further down, the surviving Whitefriars Gate and, hidden by smoke, the lofty Castle & Co (no. 43).

A general view of the Whitefriars area from mid-June 1942. Far right is the tall, gutted shell of wine merchants, Castle & Co. Many of the adjacent ruins had already been cleared away by this time. Far left, some of the Sun Buildings still stand.

The middle of St George's Street in July 1942 after further demolition. On the right, the jagged two-toned wall is all that is left of Castle & Co, recently toppled. Beyond it, the white line in the rubble is Whitefriars Passage, the gate having been pulled down.

The Cathedral, as seen from the middle of St George's Street in the late 1940s. The photographer is standing on the site of World's Stores, the grocers, at no. 47. To the left and fenced off with chestnut paling, is Whitefriars Passage.

The east end of St George's Street on 1 June 1942 with people taking stock of the devastation. Left, are the walls and collapsed rubble of Woolworth's (no. 54), London Outfitters (no 55) and blocking St George's Lane, the Coach & Horses at no 56.

Three weeks later and the clearance gangs have been at work. In the immediate foreground, a demolition lorry is parked in St George's Lane. Beyond it, some of the ruined outbuildings behind the site of the Coach and Horses, are still standing.

An intact oast and a row of partly burnt out cottages (nos 4 to 8), on the east side of St George's Lane in July 1942.

No. 13 St George's Lane (west side), an early 19th-century house that, although damaged, would be retained.

A famous view of the wasteland that was once the St George's parish in 1946. St George's Lane, with its low wooden fence, runs across a vast empty area.

St George's Gate and St George's Street on 4 June 1942. The ruins of the Sun Building are on the left, with the now familiar ruins of Castle & Co beyond. The 'no entry' sign is due to the imminent visit by the Duke Of Kent.

The Buffs march along the east end of St George's Street in 1948. Behind, is a sea of trees and shrubs, where once stood the buildings on the street's south side. Far left is the site of Jays Furnishing stores (nos 57 & 58) and the Marlowe birth place.

The once elegant houses of St George's Terrace in early July 1942. The gap that was once no 6, is the work of the demolition squad, rather than enemy action. It was claimed by contemporary observers that these gutted houses could have been restored.

A view from the same spot in the late 1940s. With the Regency terrace gone, one can see the surviving houses in St George's Lane (nos 7, 8 and 13) and part of the Simon Langton School beyond them.

A poor, yet interesting picture of demolition in progress on St George's Terrace. The Sun Buildings (left) are coming down.

St George's Terrace in the mid-1940s, its former grandeur now a distant memory.

The garden perimeter of Terrace House that once stood on St George's Terrace between the now lost Gravel Walk slope and Watling Street.

The Simon Langton Schools

THE Simon Langton Schools opened on the Whitefriars site in 1881. The boys' school had been created to replace the Blue Coat School in Stour Street, the girls' school was a new foundation.

The new school buildings, of red brick and Bath stone dressing, had re-used some materials recovered from the mansion house, demolished to make way for them. Of course, the former Augustinian friary had long since been pulled down, although there were still old mediaeval remains to be found (and discussed in a separate chapter). Both schools were strictly segregated from the start, despite them being side by side within the same walled precinct. However, this separation was relaxed slightly as the years progressed.

Success led to the schools being expanded in the following decades. In the late 1890s, a new science block was built for the boys school at the top end of Gravel Walk, and in the 1900s, a new block for the girls' school appeared at the north end of the Whitefriars site. Another major extension for the boys' school was constructed along the St George's Lane perimeter in 1914. Space was always at a premium and both schools considered leaving the Whitefriars in the years between the wars. As a temporary expedient, the boys' school purchased some ex-army huts and erected them next to the 1914 extension building. However, they became a permanent feature and lasted until the very end. In July 1931, the schools joined together to celebrate their golden jubilee. This took the form of a costumed pageant, performed on the tennis courts in the girls' section of the school grounds.

World War Two affected both schools significantly. In September 1940, half the girls school evacuated to Reading, shortly followed by the boys', half of whom decamped to Wantage in Berkshire. The school buildings suffered terribly in the 1 June 1942 raid, the Whitefriars area being situated in that quadrant of the city most affected by the bombing. Around 50 percent of the boys' school and some 90 percent of the girls' school was rendered unusable, mainly by incendiary bombs. Only a tiny portion of the original 1881 complex was unaffected. The burnt out shells were quickly demolished in the weeks that followed. Given the staggering loss, the girls' school had no choice but to leave the Whitefriars site. A temporary school was set up at Stone House along the Littlebourne Road. (This was a former mental asylum, a fact that greatly amused the Langton boys.) Eventually, the girls moved to a new purpose built complex, along the Old Dover Road, in 1951.

In the meantime, the boys' school continued in what was left at Whitefriars. In the mid to late 1940s, a series of prefabricated 'Ministry huts' were erected on the site of the blitzed and levelled buildings, to ease the accommodation problems. Life on the Whitefriars site was neither easy nor comfortable for the boys' school in these early post-war years. In the winter months, the ink would literally freeze in the ink wells.

The mid-1950s financial crisis, that scuppered the City Council's plans to redevelop the city on the basis of compulsory purchase, also held up the chance of a new Simon Langton Boys' School being built. In June 1954, the chairman of the Canterbury & District joint education committee said, with regret, that the new school would not be placed on the building programme in the near future. Deliverance finally came in November 1959, when the school relocated to a new purpose built complex constructed on their remote playing fields at Nackington. The old school buildings at Whitefriars were all demolished in June and July of 1960. This was preceded by a brief archaeological excavation in the former playground area that identified features from both the Roman and Saxon periods.

Part of the school's 1881 complex with St George's Street and the Cathedral to the right (north). The boys' school is to the left and the girls' part, partially obscured by the Langton's famous Tulip Tree, is to the right.

The north facing part of the original girls' school building and the first thing that one saw at the end of Whitefriars Passage.

An ancient vaulted chamber was broken into, when foundations for the 1914 boys' school extension were dug. The 1890s science block, also part of the boys' school, is in the background.

Participants of a costumed pageant, staged in 1931, to celebrate the jubilee of both schools. The rears of some St George's Street properties can be seen beyond the old north perimeter wall.

Furious activity at the boys' school mock elections, held in November 1935. The three candidates stood for: 'labour', 'conservatives' and fascists! Needless to say, the conservatives won. The tower of St Mary Bredin Church is visible to the left.

Real White Friars? These bones were uncovered in 1939, when air raid shelters were dug in a former orchard area within the girls' school grounds. This was situated to the west of Whitefriars Passage.

Evacuees, including Simon Langton Boys, wait at Canterbury East Station in September 1940. Their destination was Wantage in Berkshire. At about the same time, much of the Langton Girls' School evacuated to Reading.

A mixed throng of boys, girls, parents and teachers wait for the train in the sidings, to move into their platform. The evacuation trains were held here until normal scheduled services had cleared. The engines would then 'run round' and head for Berkshire.

The south side of the boy's school following the Baedeker raid of June 1942. The entire 1881 complex was burnt out. Luckily the later extensions backing on to Gravel Walk and St George's Lane survived. In all, about 50 percent of the boys' school perished.

The only part of the girls' school not to have been destroyed on the 1 June 1942, and the only surviving portion of the original 1881 buildings. With 90 percent of their school gone, the girls were forced to abandon the Whitefriars site.

The first of four parts of the official 1959 Simon Langton Boys' School photograph, the last year they were at the Whitefriars complex. Behind is the colonnaded terrace of shops, built on the south side of St George's Street in the early to mid-1950s.

The only remaining part of the original 1881 buildings, once part of the girls' school and used by the boys since 1942. Beyond and to the left is the 1939 rear extension to Marks & Spencer.

One of the former army huts brought in to supplement the school's accommodation. The surviving 1881 part of the school is to the left and on the right, a section of flint wall once thought to have been part of the mediaeval friary complex.

The other end of the above mentioned wall, situated at the end of Whitefriars Passage, an ancient right of way, once used to access the friary, then from 1881, the Simon Langton Girls' School. A new service road for the colonnade is in the foreground.

The second part of the 1959 photograph, this piece including some of the teaching staff. Behind is part of the school complex that backs on to St George's Lane and, since 1956, the bus station.

A view across the playground from the boys' school's Gravel Walk entrance, in the autumn of 1959, just prior to their relocation to Nackington. Far left, the new Pricerite supermarket is under construction.

The very north-east corner of the school grounds, with some blitz surviving buildings in St George's Lane beyond. The low building is probably a toilet block. This part of the school grounds had been used in the 1951 Festival Exhibition as a tea garden.

These army huts were installed by the boys' school, in the years between the wars, to provide much needed additional capacity. They were situated against the St George's Lane frontage, immediately south of the buildings in the top picture.

The third section of the 1959 school roll call. Behind are the buildings in the south-east corner of the site, situated at the junction of St George's Lane and Gravel Walk. They are all later extensions to the original boys' school.

The 1914 extension building to Simon Langton Boys' School, containing classrooms 15, 16 and 17 on the upper storey, with the gymnasium beneath. The gym was also used by the girls' school before 1942.

Part of the Science Block of the 1890s that backed on to the north side of Gravel Walk. This is the workshop and physics laboratory of 1897, added to the school during the tenure of headmaster William Partington-Mann.

The single-storey chemistry lab, built in 1894, is reflected in the large puddle on the empty playground, shortly after the school closed in November 1959. The prefects' room is on the far right.

The final portion of the school photograph, taken in the last summer at Whitefriars. Part of the science block is once again seen as the backdrop. The very narrow Gravel Walk could be found beyond it.

Some of the prefabricated 'ministry huts' erected in the south-west corner of the site, in the late 1940s, to allow the boys' school to struggle on at the Whitefriars site, until a new and permanent school complex could be built.

The prefects' room, situated at the west end of the science block. To the right is the school's Gravel Walk entrance, which had always only been used by the boys' school. On the other side of Gravel Walk, the premises of Drew's Coaches can be seen.

Another view of the useful, yet very basic prefabricated classrooms, used by the boys' school from the late 1940s until November 1959. Behind, is the Regency period house on the southern corner of Gravel Walk and Rose Lane.

Some of the guests who attended a lunch at the County Hotel to mark the impending opening of the new boy's school at Nackington. Centre view is Alderman Jennings, an old boy and chairman of the governors. Far right is former headmaster, Mr L.W. Myers.

The new Simon Langton Boys' School complex, at Nackington, in November 1959. It was built on a corner of the school's existing remote playing fields, situated over a mile from the Whitefriars site. The design was the work of City Architect Hugh Wilson.

Sections of a Roman tessellated floor, uncovered in one of the archaeological trenches, sunk in the former playground area at Whitefriars during May 1960.

Saxon period post holes overlay the foundations of a Roman Wall, in another of the trenches, excavated in spring 1960. It has been a long time since female archaeologists wore frocks on site!

Demolition in progress, of the former school buildings at Whitefriars, in around July 1960. Furthest right are the remains of the 1914 extension block, with some of the stripped out prefabs in front of it. Centre view is the iron skeleton of the old army huts.

The cleared Whitefriars site in late 1960, as seen from the recently constructed shops on the south side of St George's Street. Only one length of wall, part of a mediaeval friary building, has been spared. Gravel Walk can be seen far left.

The Canterbury Festival Exhibition

CANTERBURY was one of the 20 cities chosen to stage the 1951 Festival of Britain. A major part of the festival was the Canterbury Exhibition, which would tell the story of the city from earliest known times to the present and into the future. Plans for this began in June 1949 and the Whitefriars area was chosen as the site for the exhibition. This included much of the south side of St George's Street and the northern half of the Simon Langton school grounds.

The area had been devastated by the blitz, but some ancient walls that were once part of the Augustinian Whitefriars friary, were still standing (see the chapter on the friary remains). These walls were proudly displayed as part of the exhibition, as were the remains of a recently excavated Roman town house, discovered in cellars on the south side of St George's Street.

Central to the Festival Exhibition was the main pavilion, dedicated to English Christianity, Thomas Becket and pilgrimages. Other areas of the site covered the Iron Age, Roman Canterbury, the dark ages, civic Canterbury, Kent agriculture, the blitz and the future rebuilding plans for the city. The last mentioned exhibit was located in the former Simon Langton air-raid shelter complex and included a large three dimensional model of the city with the completed Wilson Plan implemented. Immediately south of the main pavilion, a monastic herb garden was laid out, using part of the old north facing friary wall as a backdrop. Another memorable feature was a huge pair of plaster hands, the right one holding a sword aloft, the left out-stretched and supporting a model of Lanfranc's Cathedral. This work represented the balance between the church and state; a recurring theme in Canterbury's history, not least in the story of Thomas Becket.

The Festival Exhibition was formally opened by the French Ambassador to England, Monsieur Rene Massigli on 11 June 1951, a gloriously sunny day. Canterbury's mediaeval Burghmote Horn was blown as a welcome to the distinguished guests. They were then escorted around the exhibition in the company of the Mayor Stanley Jennings, Alderman Barrett and the City Architect Hugh Wilson.

The exhibition closed on 12 September and shortly after, the pavilions and displays were dismantled prior to the redevelopment of the south side of St George's Street. Sadly, demolished at the same time were some of the friary remains that had been so proudly displayed during the preceding months. Some of the plaster statues from the exhibition were moved to the Dane John, but eventually crumbled away.

Devastation on the south side of St George's Street, from the gutted remains of the recently constructed Woolworth store at no 54, down to the lofty shell of Castle & Co at no 43. This would later be chosen as the site of the Festival Exhibition.

A typical late 1940s scene of the south side of St George's Street, where a recent archaeological dig had uncovered the remains of a Roman house.

The ruined weighing machine in the rubble that was once Woolworth's.

Construction in progress for the Canterbury Exhibition, viewed from the roof of Marks & Spencer. Just above centre, the end walls of the main pavilion are nearly finished. The sites of nos 37 to 42 (in the foreground) were not part of the scheme.

With the Cathedral as backdrop, men attempt to unload a huge pair of plaster hands, which will form part of a significant sculpture for the festival site.

One of the heavy plaster hands being unloaded gingerly, in the age before the Health and Safety at Work Act! Beyond is Marks & Spencer (left) and centre view, the Midland Bank building on the corner of Butchery Lane.

The then Mayor, Alderman Stanley Jennings, who in the festival booklet, expressed a hope that as a result of the Canterbury Exhibition, the world will see that the city's motto 'Ave Mater Angliae' (Hail Mother of England) is well deserved.

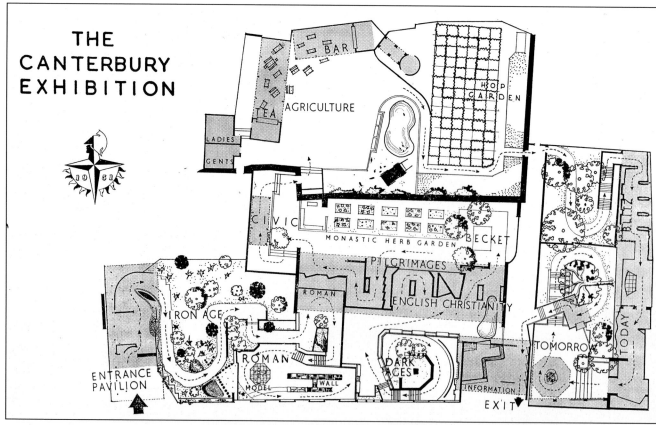

A plan of the exhibition site as published in the festival programme. The entrance pavilion (left) is near the St George's Lane junction and the exit, along Whitefriars Passage. The thickly marked walls are those containing friary remains.

The French Ambassador to England, Monsieur Massigli, listens to the city's Burghmote Horn being blown, at the opening of the Canterbury Exhibition, on 11 June 1951. His wife and the mayor also look on.

The exhibition site, as seen from St George's Terrace and overlooking the visitors temporary car park off St George's Lane. The massive scaffolding hoarding reads 'Canterbury Festival Exhibition'. Beyond it is the entrance pavilion.

A model of Roman Canterbury, based on finds up to 1951, on display in the Roman area.

The bridge that led from the 'Iron Age' area, to the Roman exhibits beneath.

The remains of a Roman 'apsidal' house on display in-situ in the Roman area. Behind is the overgrown area dedicated to the Iron Age and the linking bridge.

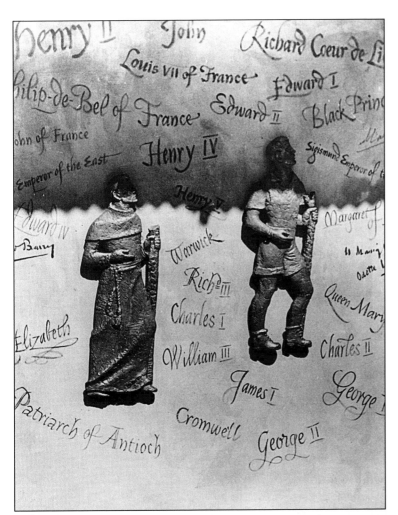

Part of a display on the south side of the main pavilion, dedicated to Pilgrimages. These two pilgrims are surrounded by facsimile signatures of the more notable figures in history to have visited Canterbury.

Plaster figures of monks and knights line the walls of the shady courtyard, dedicated to Thomas Becket. This could be found at the west end of a Monastic Herb Garden. Whitefriars Passage ran behind this brick wall.

The central sculpture of the 'Becket' area, featuring the aforementioned pair of huge plaster hands. One is holding a sword aloft, the other supports a model of Lanfranc's 11th-century cathedral. This work represented the balance between church and state.

The Becket sculpture is included once again in this view of the monastic herb garden, looking east towards the Civic Pavilion. The Whitefriars north wall, which included some mediaeval fabric, can be seen as the backdrop to the herb garden.

The south side of the Main Pavilion taken from atop a new wall next to the Civic Pavilion. The ladies in the foreground (left) are about to pass into the agricultural area. Left, are some turf-lined seats, situated at the east end of the Monastic Herb Garden.

A closer view of the civic pavilion, that featured a painting of a 13th-century council meeting, flanked by lists of every known 'Civic Servant' from 1,200 years of Canterbury history. In the foreground are the turf seats seen earlier.

The Mayor Stanley Jennings, in the company of Madame Massigli, point to the Wilson Plan Model, displayed in the 'tomorrow' area west of Whitefriars Passage. To the left, the ambassador chats with the Sheriff of Canterbury, Alderman John Barrett.

A close-up of the model of the completed Wilson Plan on display in the 'Tomorrow' area, reached via the 'blitz' exhibit, housed in the former Simon Langton air-raid shelters. It shows the Whitefriars area, as it would have appeared, developed in the 1950s scale.

The 1950s

FROM the early 1950s onwards, Canterbury City Council began to purchase compulsorily, blitzed sites across the Whitefriars area. The Wilson Development Plan had identified 33 acres of the city for which, they claimed, compulsory purchase was essential to carry out the rebuilding works. Hapless owners of the once grand terraced houses along St George's Terrace received an average of £50 payment for their blitzed and overgrown sites.

Rebuilding of our study area began in late 1951 with the construction of the first part of the colonnaded terrace of shops on the south side of St George's Street. This area had recently been used to stage the Canterbury Festival Exhibition (detailed in its own chapter). Parts of Rose Lane were widened in 1952 but the kinks were not straightened out until a further widening scheme at the end of the decade. Barrett's opened a new store in April 1954 immediately to the west of the surviving Marks & Spencer. At around the same time, the *Kentish Gazette*, whose print works were on the east side of Marks & Spencer, relocated to St George's Place.

Lack of government funding had contributed to a substantial scaling down of the City Council's compulsory purchase plans by the middle of the 1950s. Consequently, the new bus station, opened in 1956, was on a site in St George's Lane privately owned by the company. Similarly, the Sun Assurance Co were finally able to redevelop their old site in 1957 for their new Sun Building. Other development included the terrace of shops on the east side of St George's Lane, the completion of the colonnade in St George's Street and new premises for Associated Engineering in Rose Lane.

Demolition of old buildings in the study area was on a small scale in the 1950s. The only casualties were the old *Gazette* works and an early 20th-century extension to the Langton Girls' School, that needed to give way for a service road behind the new colonnaded terrace in St George's Street. No 1 Watling Street also perished in this decade.

The Simon Langton Boys' School continued to occupy their Whitefriars site until November 1959, when they finally relocated to new buildings at Nackington. This freed up a large area that would be subject to redevelopment in the 1960s.

Once again, we are about to pass through the Riding Gate and into the Whitefriars area. It is February 1957 and beyond the gate, no 1 Watling Street is gone, but no 2 still hangs on. The UR Church is completed but only its lobby is visible from here.

The site of the demolished no 1 Watling Street, with the bus station beyond, on 20 July 1957. A strike had halted all services, hence the deserted forecourt. Many pre-blitz buildings, including the Simon Langton School, are visible in this view.

The late Victorian period house at no 2 Watling Street, seen from the Dane John Gardens in February 1953. By this time, it was the office premises of various Canterbury firms.

A Catholic procession descends the slope from St George's Terrace and approaches Watling Street, en route to a service on the Dane John, during 1953.

Watling Street car park, in November 1957, after a freak gale had flattened the marquees of an agricultural show. Beyond are the terraced houses at nos 12 to 14 Watling Street and the two shops either side of the narrow junction for Rose Lane.

A veteran car taking part in a rally through Canterbury during August 1955. Behind are nos 10 to 15 Watling Street, the last being the Kent Type Writer Co Ltd shop at the Rose Lane corner. Nos 13 to 15 would perish in 1960 for an improved junction.

The bottom end of Rose Lane in April 1952, with the former Parade Chambers site (right) being prepared for road widening. The wall fragment to the left is part of the façade of the former Fountain Tap pub.

The same scene, with road widening in progress during the summer of 1952.

An earlier view of the overgrown cellars of the lost Parade Chambers, with the narrow Rose Lane bordered on either side by chestnut paling.

The St George's Street end of Rose Lane in spring 1955, by which time, road widening had been completed and redevelopment started. Right is the shop for Barrett's, opened the previous year and left, the frame for what will become Perring's.

Four years later and further road widening and straightening had taken place. Perring's was finished and right, the premises for Associated Engineering was completed. The empty plot (right) was earmarked for a new Barrett's showroom building.

The bottom end of Rose Lane, as seen from the Longmarket, in April 1952. Right, Buddleia crowds the former Rose Club site whilst left, the foundations for a widened lane are already in place. Further left, work would soon start on a shop for Barrett's.

A similar view from the mid-1950s. The new Barrett's and Associated Engineering buildings are on the left. Further up the lane, the former pre-war premises of the latter business are about to be demolished, allowing the kink in Rose Lane to be eliminated.

The redeveloped south side of St George's Street, as envisaged by the City Architects' Department in 1950. The colonnaded terrace would be closely based on a similar scheme then being built in the London borough of Poplar.

A section of the south side of St George's Street, in November 1951. Left, are the hoardings of the Festival Exhibition, closed three months earlier. Right is the site of the pre-war Mac Fisheries and behind, surviving buildings from the Simon Langton schools.

Start of work on the colonnaded 'Poplar' terrace of shops in spring 1952, following the demolition and clearance of the Festival Exhibition. The frames for what will become 16, 18 and 20 are seen here. No 18 would become the new Mac Fisheries.

The completed first phase of the colonnade, in October 1952. Note that it has been set well back from the existing street line to allow St George's Street to be widened. In the foreground are the broken up remains of the entrance pavilion from the exhibition.

The entire south side of St George's Street in November 1952, with road widening in progress. Beyond the new terrace, the shed-like office premises of the *Kentish Gazette* can be made out. Far left are the walls and buildings of the Simon Langton Boys' School.

The completed colonnade from ground level. New occupants are: Phillip Bros shoes (16), Mac Fisheries (18), Manfield & Sons (20), Scotch Wool Stores (22), Dorothy Perkins (24), Mount's florist (26), Paige Gowns Ltd (28) and Lipton's (30).

A privately owned shop was added to the east end of the colonnade in 1953. Built by Wiltshier's, the first occupants were Jays The Furnishers (no 32).

St George's Street in 1954 with road widening completed and new shops on either side.

A new 25ft street lamp being installed outside the old *Kentish Gazette* premises, in January 1954.

A Linotype machine being removed from the *Gazette's* old St George's Street premises, during the relocation to St George's Place, in February 1954. A snow flurry does not seem to have dampened the spirits of the cheerful *Kentish Gazette* crew.

Further equipment being moved from no 8 St George's Street during February 1954. The old print works are on the right, with part of the Langton school visible behind. The yard area was once the Conservative Club, which was a blitz victim.

Boy Scouts and Wolf Cubs from the Canterbury, Whitstable and Herne Bay associations, parade along St George's Street, on St George's Day, in April 1954. The new shops at nos 16 to 32 (evens only) provide the back-drop.

Scoutmaster Colin Trussold, did not let injury prevent him from taking part in the St George's Day Parade and marched on crutches. Behind, demolition of a pre-war building, pictured earlier, is to allow for a service road to be made for the colonnade.

The colonnaded terrace of shops being extended to fill the gap on the south side of St George's Street, in spring 1955. This was made possible following the relocation of the *Kentish Gazette* and the demolition of their old premises.

The colonnade with Christmas lights twinkling, in late 1955. The clean lines of the new development can be appreciated in this view, especially with no vehicles present. Today, vistas are not possible because of the trees and other street clutter.

The Revd Donald Soper, head of the Methodist Church in Britain, addresses a spell bound gathering on a bomb site in St George's Lane, during the winter of 1952, through to 53. Behind, other onlookers crowd the slope up to St George's Terrace.

Another view of the Methodist gathering just off St George's Lane, this one taken from St George's Terrace. St George's Tower can just be made out in the gloom, as can the building site for the new Jays Furnisher's shop next to the end of the colonnade.

The area east of St George's Lane being prepared for redevelopment, in August 1955. This will include a terrace of shops and new Sun Building.

The foundations in place for a new terrace of shops on the east side of St George's Lane, during April 1956.

The new terrace of shops at nos 5 to 17 (odds only) St George's Lane, all but complete in July 1957. The first occupant is Electronics (Canterbury) Ltd at no 11. Far left, part of the new Sun Building is also visible.

A Kent Fire Brigade exercise taking part on the recently vacated cattle market area of Upper Bridge Street, in the summer of 1955. Beyond St George's Terrace, the new bus station is taking shape alongside older buildings, including Simon Langton School.

Part of the city wall between Riding Gate and St George's Gate, as it appeared in April 1957. St George's Terrace, now devoid of all buildings, runs along the top of this stretch of wall. Beyond, is the bus station office building.

One of two facsimile defensive bastions being constructed along the length of city wall beneath St George's Terrace, in April 1958. The width of Watling Street prevented a third being built, next to Riding Gate, on the foundations of its mediaeval predecessor.

An aerial view of St George's Lane and the south side of St George's Street, in the summer of 1959, with much redevelopment completed. The Simon Langton buildings (bottom left) prevent the re-routing of St George's Lane, at least for now.

A site being prepared at the top end of Rose Lane, in January 1959, for a new garage premises for Southern Autos Ltd. They had recently taken over from Philpott's.

Within a few weeks, the skeleton of the new garage premises was complete.

The opening ceremony of Southern Auto's complex in Rose Lane, being addressed by the Mayor, Alderman W.S. Bean, in May 1959. Behind are Mrs Bean and the company's managing director, Mr J.A. Dodd. The garage later became Marlowe Motors.

The Non-conformist Church

THE oldest version of the non-conformist chapel in Watling Street within living memory, is the Countess of Huntingdon's Connexion Congregational Church, built in 1863. This stone and brick church with its lofty gable and twin porches is familiar from old postcard views.

The church escaped the ravages of the Baedeker raid on 1 June 1942, only to be gutted by incendiary bombs in one of the minor raids in the days that followed. The roofless and fire damaged shell was not demolished and the potential to repair was considered. However, the matter was settled on 31 October when the church's façade was destroyed by a high explosive bomb during the infamous daylight raid.

In 1943, the church decided to join with the mainstream Congregationalists who worshipped from a Victorian church in Guildhall Street. Their church, although useable, was not in the best of condition, so a joint decision was made to rebuild on the Watling Street site. By the end of the 1940s, the Guildhall Street church had been sold to Lefevre's for conversion into a shop and a prefabricated church building had appeared on the Watling Street site.

The construction of a permanent replacement Congregational Church began in 1954. The partially built church was dedicated in a solemn ceremony on 19 March 1955, an occasion that also included the laying of three commemorative stones by senior churchmen.

Sadly, the run of bad luck that had begun in 1942 was to continue. A dispute arose in 1955, between the various church factions and the contractors over payment for the church foundations. Building work stopped, the weeds gathered and the scaffolding rusted for the next year. Once the dispute was settled, construction resumed and by October 1958 the external work had been completed.

In the early 1970s, the Congregationalists joined with the Presbyterians to form the United Reformed Church. Over the years, the 1950s church had become a familiar landmark, with its gentle modernist lines and clear influences from Coventry Cathedral, particularly in the angled vertical windows in the south elevation. However, it is the large wooden cross on the frontage that many people recall.

As soon as the Whitefriars redevelopment was first mooted, it became clear that the church was doomed. Its destruction occurred in the spring of 2001. Sadly, the three commemorative foundation stones and the large wooden cross were destroyed along with the rest of the building. What a contrast to the solemn consecration ceremony some 46 years before. The stones were so carefully laid, so carelessly discarded.

The handsome symmetrical façade of the 1863 Countess of Huntingdon's Connexion Church, on the north side of Watling Street, pictured in the early 20th century. It was the third version of the church on the same site.

The church's imposing façade following gutting by the incendiary fires of the June 1942 raids. Although the roof and interior were gone, the shell was sound and escaped the post blitz demolition purge. It is probable that repair was being considered.

The remains of the frontage being pulled down by hand following the daylight raid of 31 October 1942, when a high explosive bomb devastated this part of Watling Street.

A new 'temporary' Congregational Church, recently erected on the Watling Street site, in 1949. By this time, the Countess of Huntingdon worshippers had joined with the Congregationalists from Guildhall Street.

By June 1954, the surrounding bomb site vegetation was beginning to envelope the temporary church. More importantly, construction work for a new permanent Congregational Church had started alongside.

Mr Clissold G Larkinson, chairman of the trustees on behalf of the Countess of Huntingdon's Connexion, leads a small procession to the official stone laying ceremony at the new Congregational Church, on Saturday 19 March 1955.

The second of three foundation stones being laid by the moderator of the Southern province, the Revd W. Andrew James. Bricklayers from the contractors, Richard Costain, look on anxiously.

Worshippers gathered round the half built church, whilst the Revd L. Criddle of Tunbridge Wells, says the prayer of dedication on 19 March 1955.

A close up study of the worshippers from the joined congregations, who attended the stone laying ceremony and dedication prayers for their new building.

A veteran car rally makes its way up Watling Street in August 1955. Of more interest is the backdrop featuring the cottages at nos 7 to 15 Watling Street (demolished between 1960 & 1965) and the partially built Congregational Church.

Work halted on the construction of the new church, as seen in March 1956, following a dispute between two undisclosed parties over the amount spent on the foundations. No building work had taken place since May 1955!

External work on the new Congregational Church finally completed, in October 1958. It was destined to become one of Canterbury's best loved post-war buildings.

The Mayor and Mayoress, Cllr and Mrs Herbert Buckworth, attending a Christmas party for 'Canterbury's blind folk and their sighted guides', in December 1968. It took place at the Congregational Hall, adjacent to the church in Watling Street.

The, by now, United Reformed Church on a typical Sunday morning, in the early 1990s. The office block, Watling House (left) had replaced the cottages in 1966 and both were dwarfed by the multi-storey car park in 1969.

Vandalism, desecration or progress? The sad sight of the United Reformed Church under demolition, on 19 April 2001. Sadly, neither the familiar wooden cross on the façade, nor the three foundation stones were rescued from the destruction.

What Remained of the Augustinian Whitefriars?

UNTIL as recently as 1941, a number of surviving elements from the mediaeval Augustinian friary could be found across the Whitefriars area. Unlike the former Christ Church Priory, the Blackfriars and perhaps the Greyfriars, no upstanding buildings remained from the Whitefriars friary. However, there was enough evidence to establish that a mediaeval foundation had existed here. So why does nothing remain today?

The Simon Langton Boys' and Girls' Schools were established here in 1881 and both schools were extremely proud of their friary relics. In fact every day, the girls had to pass through Whitefriars Gate in St George's Street to get to school. The gate, which had been heavily restored in 1937, contained quantities of red brick and re-used Caen stone in its fabric, suggesting an earlier rebuild or extensive repair.

Beyond the gate was Whitefriars Passage that ran between the St George's Street properties and on to the school site. Towards the end of the passage, and before a second pair of wrought iron gates, a flint wall appeared on the left. Straight away, a stone jambed gothic doorway could be found within this wall. This is widely believed to have been the original west door of the Whitefriars Church. Beyond the gate, the flint wall continued its course south. It was of substantial construction, with a small stone dressed plinth and neatly knapped flint facing. Within this stretch of the wall could be seen a small blocked window and a second much larger three-lighted window, also blocked up, but with much perpendicular gothic stone tracery still in situ. This entire wall was likely to have been the remains of the west wall of the church and to the south of it, the wall of an adjacent building, perhaps from the west range of a small cloister arrangement.

Another old wall ran parallel to St George's Street and divided the school grounds from the shop back gardens. This was largely of post-mediaeval construction, but possibly built on the foundations of the north wall of the Whitefriars Church. However, part of this wall did contain mediaeval fabric above ground. Two

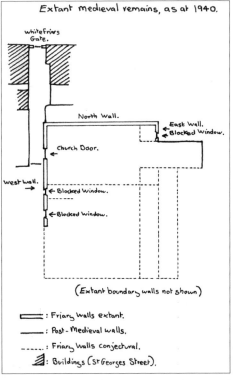

Extant medieval remains, as at 1940.

Whitefriars Gate.

North Wall.

East Wall.
Blocked Window.

Church Door.

West Wall.

← Blocked Window.

← Blocked Window.

(Extant boundary walls not shown)

▭ : Friary Walls extant.
━━ : Post-Medieval walls.
----- : Friary Walls conjectural.
▨ : Buildings (St Georges Street).

thirds along its length, this wall turned 90 degrees south for a few yards before turning again to resume its easterly course. Between the two angles, the short stretch of wall that resulted contained a stone jambed gothic window, blocked up in brick, but sitting on a well preserved stone dressed and flint faced plinth. The accompanying plan interprets this feature as being the east end wall of the north aisle, at the point the church narrowed to form a chancel. However, recent archaeological investigations suggest that this feature could have been the east wall of a chapel, projecting from the north wall of the church.

Apart from these fascinating remains, a substantial length of the Whitefriars precinct boundary wall had survived, albeit much altered in the intervening years. The best preserved length curved from Rose Lane into Gravel Walk and up to the entrance used by the boys' school.

Destruction of these relics began in June 1942. The Whitefriars Gate had survived the Baedeker Raid that caused the destruction of much of St George's Street's south side. However, it was demolished, probably by accident, in the overly thorough post-blitz clearance operation. Then in late 1951, having been proudly displayed as cherished history remains in the Festival Exhibition (see that chapter), the west church door and the entire north wall, were destroyed in advance of the rebuilding of St George's Street. The boundary wall perished in 1960, when the redundant Simon Langton Boys' School was cleared away.

This just left the remaining section of west wall, too obviously of genuine mediaeval origin to have been demolished in either the 1951 or 1960 clearances. By now though, it was marooned in the middle of a massive surface car park. Sadly, this too was pulled down in around 1970, prior to the construction of the Whitefriars Shopping arcade.

So in answer to the question at the beginning, it may be that Canterbury was too spoilt by its wealth of substantial mediaeval church buildings, to have given these fragments much priority, or to have altered the rebuilding plans to incorporate them.

Whitefriars Gate, of uncertain date, on the south side of St George's Street in 1941. At this time, the gate and passage beyond accessed not only the girls' school, but also a city air-raid shelter.

St George's Street on the morning of 1 June 1942, with firemen damping down the remains of the buildings on its south side. The undamaged Whitefriars Gate can be seen between the two pairs of fire fighters.

The far end of Whitefriars Passage on a snowy day in the early years of the 20th century. The school buildings are ahead to the right. On the left is the west wall, (i.e. running north to south) mostly of mediaeval date. Note the doorway, far left.

A 1930s period drawing of the ancient doorway in the west wall. It is substantially built with stone jambs and widely believed to have been the original west door of the friary church.

The short stretch of east facing wall, between the two 90 degree turns in the main north wall. The blocked window (left) sits on a substantial stone dressed plinth of undoubted mediaeval origin.

A close-up of the stone jambed gothic window, blocked up in brick. This was once either the window at the east end of the church's north aisle, or a window in the east wall of a chapel that projected from the north wall of the church.

A 1959 view of the southernmost blocked up mediaeval window in the west wall, at this time, standing in the Simon Langton playground. Although partially obscured by the tree, the intact perpendicular stone tracery can clearly be seen.

The other side (the original inner face) of the west wall, as seen from the Simon Langton playground, in late 1959. The outlines of both blocked windows can be made out. The apertures on the inner face would have been splayed and therefore much larger.

The first of four pictures of the Whitefriars perimeter wall, taken in early 1960, just prior to its demolition. Here the ominous site of a pneumatic drill's air pipe along Rose Lane, means that work is about to begin.

The mediaeval precinct wall, as it turns the corner from Rose Lane to run along the north side of Gravel Walk. At the far end of Gravel Walk, can be seen the 1890s and 1914 extension buildings for the boys' school.

Demolition work in progress, at the western end of the school grounds. Far right is the 1939 rear extension to Marks & Spencer that occupied the site of Rose Square. Left is the new Perring store on the other side of a widened Rose Lane.

A close up of the inner face of the precinct or perimeter wall, showing post-mediaeval repair work in both brick and re-cycled Caen stone. The upper brick courses of the wall were, of course, also later work.

A mid-1960s picture of the outer face of the west wall which, by this time, was the only fragment of mediaeval Whitefriars that remained. Riceman's looms up in the distance.

A final view of the wall's inner face, against which cars were able to 'pay and display'. The position of the demolished west church door, would have been furthest right. The rest of the wall had gone by 1970.

Cityscapes

BEING the tallest building in central Canterbury, the Cathedral has proved to be a good vantage point from which to photograph the rest of the city. Pictures have been taken from all directions, but none are more interesting than those of the Whitefriars area.

In the years from 1942 to 1975, changes occurred almost daily in this part of Canterbury. There must have been views of Whitefriars captured in the years before the blitz, but I have never been able to find any. Therefore, the following sequence starts with Anthony Swaine's famous post-bombing picture, taken at around 11am on 1 June 1942. Subsequent images record the post-blitz clearance programme, the

Buddleia covered acres of the late 1940s and the rebuilding of the area over the following three decades. Also sadly missing from the chronology is a photograph taken from the Cathedral during the Festival Exhibition of 1951. However, those pictures in the chapter especially dedicated to the subject, should more than make up for the loss.

Any Canterbury photographer will tell you that attempting to take a photograph in a southerly direction is always a problem because of the sun, even at its dullest. Therefore, it is to the credit of the various people responsible for the following views, that they have turned out so well.

It is 11am on 1 June 1942. Anthony Swaine's famous view of the smouldering south-east quadrant of the city, following the main Baedeker raid. Steam from the damping down process mingles with smoke in the air above Whitefriars.

August 1942 and the post-blitz demolition and clearance programme is in progress. Most of St George's Street has been levelled, although damaged buildings still stand in St George's Lane. Note the grounded barrage balloon in the Langton playground.

A typical late 1940s scene with the few remaining buildings surrounded by numerous overgrown bomb sites. Surviving cottages in St George's Lane can just be made out, as can the remaining buildings of the Simon Langton complex.

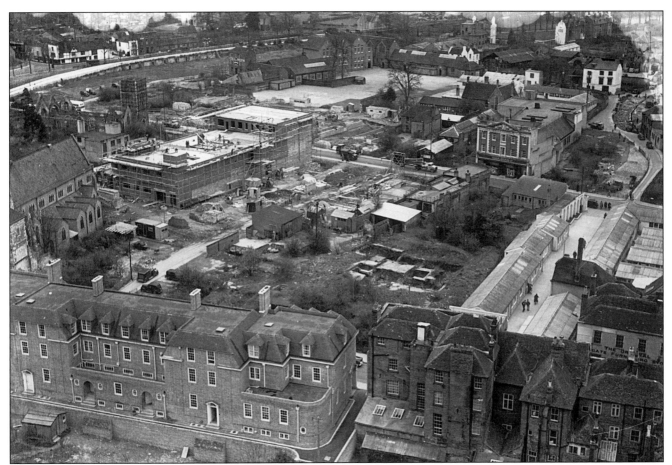

Spring 1952 and the rebuilding has begun. On the Whitefriars area, the Canterbury Festival has come and gone. Foundations for the new shops on the south side of St George's Street are being laid down alongside the old *Kentish Gazette* premises.

September 1952 and the St George's Street colonnade is taking shape. Far right, Rose Lane has been widened but not yet straightened out. Demolition in advance of the bus station construction has taken place in St George's Lane and Watling Street.

New buildings in evidence on the south side of St George's Street in May 1954. Note Barrett's next to Marks & Spencer and Jay's at the east end of the colonnade. By now the *Kentish Gazette* had relocated and their old premises had been demolished.

A dull day in the summer of 1960. The bus station and new shops can be seen in St George's Lane. The colonnaded terrace now extends right to Marks & Spencer. The Simon Langton School has relocated and the old buildings are being pulled down.

A much changed scene in summer 1964. Riceman's has appeared and the former Langton grounds are a huge car park. Both Gravel Walk and Rose Lane have been widened although old buildings still hang on between Gravel Walk and Watling Street.

February 1968 and the last pre-war building has gone (except Marks & Spencer). Surface car parking now covers much of the Whitefriars area. Watling House, between Marlowe Motors and the Congregational Church, is a new arrival since the last view.

A deserted Canterbury, probably on a Sunday in May 1969. Construction work on the infamous multi-storey car park is at an advanced stage. A tree immediately behind the colonnaded terrace means that the last bit of mediaeval Whitefriars wall still hangs on.

September 1975 and the modernist rebuilding of Canterbury is completed. The Whitefriars shopping arcade, seen here soaring above the more discreet St George's Street shops, was the last significant development of this phase in the city's history.

The Bus Station

IN THE early 1950s, the bus station operated by East Kent Road Car Co Ltd was on a small site at the Westgate end of St Peter's Place. An extension to the bus station could be found in nearby Station Road West, alongside the blitzed site of the company's office.

Having to use two sites was far from satisfactory, besides which, the City Council were threatening to compulsorily purchase the St Peter's Place site for their ring road plans. As mentioned earlier, the Wilson Development Plan had identified 33 acres of Canterbury that would need to be purchased compulsorily, in order to make the rebuilding of the city effective. Much of the land to be acquired was in the blitzed Whitefriars quadrant, but other areas, such as around the proposed ring road circuit were also identified. Quite understandably, East Kent were very annoyed at having their bus station taken away and with nowhere else being offered to them for relocation. The bus company had their eye on the strip of blitzed land between St George's Lane and St George's Terrace. However, the council had ruled out the siting of a bus station within the city walls.

Given the stalemate, East Kent had no choice but to resist the purchase of their St Peter's Place site. With their ring road plans potentially held up for an unknown period of time, the City Council relented and agreed to an exchange of land with the bus company. Ironically, the only available and suitable land in the City Council's ownership was the site to the east of St George's Lane. This had been acquired in pieces by them, on a compulsory purchase basis, in the early 1950s. The matter was settled by the Minister of Transport who insisted that the new bus station be situated inside the city walls.

Construction work got under way in 1955. At the official stone laying ceremony for the new bus station office block, the Mayor Alderman H.P. Dalton and East Kent Chairman, Mr R.T. Beddow, officially buried their differences. The new bus station opened in May 1956.

Plans for the Whitefriars Development Scheme included the re-modelling of the, by now, Stagecoach owned bus station. Demolition of the mid-1950s version of the bus station began in November 1999 and at the time of writing, the new re-modelled station was up and running.

Blitzed damaged cottages on the east side of a very narrow St George's Lane, in July 1942. At the far end of the terrace is an oast house. Both oast and damaged houses would shortly be demolished. Only nos 7 and 8 (mid view) would remain for now.

The rear of the St George's Lane oast from St George's Terrace, after much demolition had taken place in the latter thoroughfare. Note the unconventional drying towers. The blast damage to the roof was more than enough justification for demolition!

The rarely pictured sloping section of Gravel Walk, as it descended from St George's Terrace at roughly mid point. At ground level, Gravel Walk met the junction for St George's Lane, close to the 1914 Simon Langton extension building seen here.

No 1 Watling Street, the former Dane John Academy, being demolished in about 1951. This was in preparation for the building of the bus station. In its latter years, this late Georgian period house had been used by the Inland Revenue as offices.

The Riding Gate Inn coming down in January 1955, to make way for the Riding Gate Roundabout. Although part of the ring road plans, the roundabout's construction was being brought forward to ease access to the forth-coming bus station.

A charming cardboard model of the £70,000 bus station scheme and proposed shops in St George's Lane, dating from February 1955. The station's first floor office was being proportioned and coloured to match the side elevation of an East Kent coach.

An informal view prior to the official stone laying ceremony at the bus station site, on 10 May 1955. On the left, East Kent's chairman, Mr R.T. Beddow, shares a joke with the Mayor, Alderman H.P. Dawton, who is holding the spirit level.

Mr Beddow addresses the gathering at the stone laying ceremony. Note the young female journalist, far left. The ceremony was the happy ending to a long dispute between the City Council and bus company over the siting of the bus station.

Construction work getting under way in spring 1955. By now the Gravel Walk slope to St George's Terrace had been eliminated. Note the remains of a Roman city wall bastion, far right, and the cellars of lost houses being covered by the new bus station wall.

Bus station construction in progress, as seen from St George's Terrace, in June 1955. Amazingly, an old house at No 13 St George's Lane (left) still manages to hang on.

Workers from contractors Richard Costain Ltd, smooth the concrete of the new bus station forecourt, in June 1955.

The first day of operation for the new bus station, in May 1956. Two of East Kent's 1953 Guy Arab IV double deckers (known as 'GFNs', after their registration numbers) can be seen in the company of earlier vehicles. The new office building shows up well.

The good humoured picket line of East Kent employees, at the station's Watling Street exit, in July 1957. This was a countrywide pay strike, where £1 per week more had been asked for, but only 3s (15p) offered. Union chiefs described it as an insult.

One of the bus company's 12 new continental touring coaches, outside the bus station buildings, in May 1964. Their luxury bodywork could accommodate 34 passengers. They lasted in service until 1978.

The bus station, towards the Watling Street end, in the winter of 1968. To the right, cars are parked on a demolition site, soon to become the extension for St George's Lane. At this time, the lane only ran from St George's Street to Gravel Walk.

The old bus station office building being demolished on 1 December 1999. The useful clock had been blanked over sometime before. The new station buildings are of an interesting post-modernist design, although there is no external clock in evidence.

Barrett's Stores

WHEN brothers John and Reg Barrett returned from their wartime duties in 1945, they found their late father's motor car and electrical business scattered across the city and operating from damaged or makeshift premises.

Consolidation and modernisation began in the early 1950s. Building work for a new general shop began on the south side of St George's Street in the winter of 1952 through to 1953. The site chosen was that immediately to the west of the surviving Marks & Spencer store, which had been occupied by the former Canterbury Club and part of the Parade Chambers in the pre-war years.

The other half of the Parade Chambers site had recently been taken up by the widening of Rose Lane. The new shop was officially opened on 22 April 1954 by TV personality David Nixon, then known mostly for his appearances on the programme *What's My Line*.

Many of us will remember Barrett's in the late 1950s and 1960s, with its electrical goods, records, prams, bikes and in particular the toy department.

This was overseen by Reg Barrett. Brother John was responsible for the car side of the business that had consolidated in new workshops behind their St Peter's Street property in the mid-1950s.

By the late 1950s, John's son Geoffrey and Reg's eldest son Douglas had joined the family business. At the same time, Barrett's wanted to further expand both its retail and vehicle business. The solution was a new building in Rose Lane that combined a ground floor car showroom with two floors of shop space. Completed by October 1960, the new premises was to be found on a corner plot between the radically realigned junction of Rose Lane with Gravel Walk. In fact, the new building spanned the route of the old narrow Rose Lane.

In the late 1970s, new car showrooms were built at the St Peter's Street site. That and the contraction of the shop side of the business ultimately led to the abandonment of the 1960 Rose Lane premises. The 1954 shop was let to C. & H. Fabrics and finally in 2000, the 1960 building was demolished for the Whitefriars Development Scheme.

Dawn on 1 June 1942 and firemen tackle the blaze at the corner of St George's Street and Rose Lane. Smoke rises from the pile of charred timbers that once was the Parade Chambers. Behind are the blackened façade of the former Canterbury Club and the undamaged Marks & Spencer.

The Buddleia covered void on the corner between Rose Lane (left) and St George's Street, a typical late 1940s view. To the right is the back of the surviving Marks & Spencer store.

Brothers John (left) and Reg (right) Barrett discuss plans for their new store on the Rose Lane-St George's Street corner plot. Note the detailed model of each floor level that allowed them to plan the internal layout in exact detail.

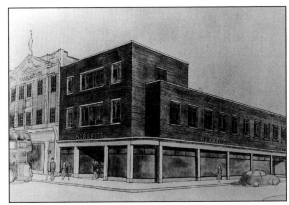

An artists impression, dating from the early 1950s, depicting the proposed new Barrett's store.

Building work in progress, towards the end of 1953.

The new Barrett's store nearing completion, in the early months of 1954. To the left is the familiar façade of Marks & Spencer and beyond that, the *Kentish Gazette* print works. To the right is Rose Lane that had been widened some two years earlier.

TV personality David Nixon speaking at the opening ceremony for the new store, on 22 April 1954. The line up (left to right) is: Mr C. Burgess (secretary), Mr H.G. Williams (director), the Mayor Alderman H.P. Dalton, David Nixon and Reg Barrett.

David Nixon cuts the ribbon and declares the bazaar open, following the inaugural ceremony. The young man immediately behind the TV star is Reg Barrett's eldest son Geoffrey, who would soon 'join the firm'.

Women and children alike eagerly crowd round the star of *What's My Line?* to obtain autographs. John Barrett had not been able to attend the opening of his store as he was recovering from a serious illness, thought to have been brought on by overwork.

David Nixon generously signs more autographs on the counter in the toy department. Note the model railway. Mr Nixon had remarked that the atmosphere of Canterbury and its people had 'got him' in a way he had never experienced before.

A mid-1950s view of the record department, in an age when a young person was just as likely to purchase a Jimmy Young record as one by Elvis Presley!

The Barrett's first floor radio and television department, 'tastefully displayed to help you make your choice'.

An external view of the Barrett's store in the late 1950s. This was at the time when John's son Geoffrey and Reg's eldest son Douglas had just joined the family business and plans to expand both retail and vehicle sides of the company were being made.

A mid-1940s view of the mid-point of Rose Lane, near its junction with Gravel Walk (right). The rear of the 1939 extension to Marks & Spencer is visible to the right. In 1960, the area, centre view, would be used to build a new Barrett's showroom.

A February 1960 picture, from almost the same spot as the one above, shows a small CND march turn the corner of a much widened and re-aligned Rose Lane. Behind the wooden fence, the building of the new Barrett's car showroom building has begun.

Father and son, Reg and Geoffrey Barrett, discuss plans for the new showroom.

The side elevation of the new building, with the Cathedral's Bell Harry Tower reflected in its huge plate glass windows.

The new car showrooms for Barretts Automobiles Ltd, in October 1961. A display of new Rover cars for 1961, is already in place. The architect for the new structure was Mr John Clague and the building contractors, Richard Costain Ltd.

A family group of (left to right) Douglas, John, Geoffrey and Reg Barrett, discuss the merits of a new Land Rover in the Rose Lane showroom, sometime in the early 1960s.

Brothers Reg and John share a joke with a children's record player and an elderly cylinder player, in 1962. Sadly, John was to die in 1971 and his brother Reg, in October 1985. By this time, the fourth generation of Barrett's, Paul and Shaun had joined the firm.

The former Barrett's showroom building, on 20 February 1998, by now occupied by Goldsmiths jewellers and the TSB bank. The building was let go following the contraction of the retail business and the opening of new showrooms in St Peter's Street.

20 May 2000, and demolition of the former Barrett's showroom, built in 1960, is in an advanced stage. Soon the basement would be back-filled and the construction of a new HSBC bank building begun.

The 1960s

THE first significant event in the Whitefriars area during this decade, was the demolition of the closed Simon Langton Boys School, in the summer of 1960. At the same time, most of the ancient mediaeval precinct wall was destroyed at the same time. This freed up a vast area for both redevelopment and road widening.

For the most part, the new buildings of the 1960s would dwarf those put up in the previous decade. Not only was the importance of the correct scale forgotten, but also the architectural styles were more aggressively modernist. However, at the beginning of the decade, new Whitefriars buildings continued to respect the mediaeval scale of the rest of the city, such as Barrett's new showroom building finished in October 1960 and the Pricerite supermarket opened at about the same time. (The Coach & Horses pub from 1963 could also be said to have had a 1950s scale.) The first large scale development was Riceman's off St George's Lane, finished in 1962, which resem-

bled a massive land locked channel ferry boat. In the same year, both St George's Lane and Gravel Walk were considerably widened on to the former school precinct, the latter planned to be the first stretch of a cross-city relief road.

Extensive demolition of old properties took place in 1965 on the block between Gravel Walk and Watling Street. This created acres of new, albeit temporary, surface car parking. In fact, by the mid-1960s, much of the undeveloped Whitefriars area was a surface car park, which, coupled with the adjacent Marlowe car park, gave the impression of a sea of cars.

Watling House, an extension to Marlowe Motors, replaced a terrace of old cottages near the Rose Lane-Watling Street junction in 1966. Then in 1968, work began on the controversial multi-storey car park, which is discussed in its own chapter. By the end of the decade, plans for another massive modernist building at Whitefriars, the Civic Centre, were unrealised (see that chapter) and unlikely to proceed.

A mid-1960s view of our gateway to the Whitefriars area, the Riding Gate. The section of the city wall to the left had collapsed at the beginning of the decade, and by now, the Riding Gate itself was also declared unsafe.

An early 1960s drawing of no 2 Watling Street, by the then City Architect, John Berbiers. Occupied by Frank Cooper Ltd as offices, this former house was subject to a compulsory purchase order in 1962. Demolition took place three years later.

The site of no 2 Watling Street, in the winter of 1968 through to 1969. Cars are parked on the narrow strip of land destined to become the extension to St George's Lane. Far left, construction of the multi-storey car park is in progress.

A gathering of nearly 70 Ford Anglias in the Watling Street Car Park, for the Invicta Motor's sponsored 'family treasure trove', in March 1962. Participants forged round the Kent countryside, gathering scraps of information, village by village, to obtain points.

A more normal day in the Watling Street car park, in about 1963. Comparison to the 1950s view in Chapter Seven, will show the amount of demolition that had occurred by this time. The cottages at nos 11 and 12 Watling Street can be seen to the right.

Demolition in progress of nos 15 down to 13 Watling Street, in early 1961, to improve the junction into Rose Lane (left). The remaining six properties in the terrace (nos 7 to 12) lasted until 1965.

The rear of the terrace at nos 7 to 15 Watling Street, as seen from Rose Lane in early 1961. Demolition of 13 to 15 is under way. It is clear from this view that before the October 1942 blitz, the terrace of houses once continued along the Rose Lane frontage.

The corner of Watling Street into Rose Lane, in the spring of 1967. By this time, all the old properties had gone, and the two roads in question considerably widened. The new Watling House development now occupied the corner plot, albeit set well back.

Marlowe Motor's in Rose Lane during 1968. To the right is Watling House, completed in 1966, a development that included ground floor car showrooms, as well as office space. The whole complex would be demolished in spring 2001.

A desolate scene looking west from the bus station in August 1962. To the left is the narrow Gravel Walk, soon to be widened on to much of this area. The remaining land in the foreground, would be reserved for the new Coach and Horses pub.

A very similar view, dating from October 1965, following the widening of Gravel Walk and the demolition of all the older properties. Gravel Walk was destined to become the first stage of a cross-city relief road, but ended up being the only part built.

Demolition rubble from the old Simon Langton school buildings is piled up all around in this August 1962 view. Beyond is the bus station, completed in 1956, and far left, the edge of the recently completed Riceman's store.

The same site, following the completion of the new Coach and Horses public house. This was the replacement for the pub lost in the June 1942 blitz.

The frontage of the Coach and Horses, from St George's Lane, in 1965. This was taken as part of Edward Wilmot's comprehensive city pub survey.

Senior staff from Marks & Spencer, with some of the surprise Christmas parcels they were about to deliver to 13 old people in Canterbury, in mid-December 1962. Some of these ladies also feature in the Duke of Kent picture, seen in Chapter Four.

The surface car park on the north side of Gravel Walk, full to capacity in May 1968. Until 1960, the site was occupied by the Simon Langton Boys' School. Far right, is part of the then remaining mediaeval wall from the Whitefriars Friary.

The elegantly curved façade of the Pricerite Supermarket, on the corner of St George's Lane and St George's Street, in October 1961. Note the modernist detailing to the narrow section facing St George's Street (right).

Staff from Pricerite's demonstrate the use of the box, where shoppers could donate their Greenshield stamps to the Canterbury Lions Club if they desired. It is January 1966. Note the large quantities of 'hard' toilet paper on the shelves behind.

An aerial view of the bus station and St George's Lane area, in 1961. The building of Riceman's is under way and the top end of St George's Lane has been developed, but the lane has yet to be reconnected to Gravel Walk, still at this time barely 8ft wide.

The 'top of the town', as local people always referred to this location, in August 1969. The post war redevelopment of the area had now largely been completed, with the exception of the Whitefriars Shopping Scheme, to follow early in the next decade.

Riceman's

BY 1950, when Fred Riceman came to Kent, he had already amassed a great deal of experience in the retail business, working for other people. Now the Riceman family were going it alone with three newly opened stores in Whitstable, Herne Bay and Deal.

Throughout the 1950s, Fred and his family had their eyes firmly fixed on Canterbury, the principal shopping centre in north-east Kent. The dream was to open a brand new department store in the most prestigious part of the city. The dream finally came true in the early 1960s, when the former Simon Langton Boys School site was cleared and its redevelopment planned.

Construction for the new Canterbury Riceman's began in 1961. The new building would front St George's Lane but was set well back to allow the former lane to be widened into a dual carriageway. When building work was nearing completion, there was a traditional topping off ceremony where family members and representatives from the construction firm Costain's, posed for pictures on the roof. Fred also organised a party in the basement, which was completed but not yet fitted out, to thank the workforce, who had pulled out all the stops to keep to the planned opening date of September 1962 firmly on schedule.

The Riceman's official opening was an elaborate affair. Prior to the ceremony, an historical pageant was held in the neighbouring streets featuring characters from Canterbury's history. This was marred only by the persistent rain.

Then, 17-year-old Miss Elizabeth Riceman performed the cutting of the ribbon ceremony and, following a speech by Fred, the crowds poured in. Honoured guests made their way up to the rooftop Grace and Favour Restaurant, which was run by experienced restaurateurs Mr and Mrs Norman Grace.

In March 1963, there was a major and potentially disastrous set back. The rooftop restaurant caught fire. Flames could be seen erupting from the store's roof and a crowd of spectators gathered along St George's Terrace. Fortunately, the fire was contained and within days, the rest of the shop re-opened. Following repairs, television and radio personality David Jacobs performed the official re-opening ceremony.

Riceman's later opened other premises in Canterbury and greatly expanded their floor space when they extended into the new Whitefriars Shopping Centre in the early 1970s. At the time of writing, the Riceman's complex was the only thing awaiting demolition for the Whitefriars Development Scheme.

The early 19th-century house at No. 13 St George's Lane in late 1959, by this time containing various small businesses, including SEREDE radio repairs and Souvenir Sound Recording Co. It would be demolished in 1960 to allow St George's Lane to be re-routed past the bus station (left).

The bus station on the evening of 26 October 1958. Buses that have finished their day's work are parked in the middle, whilst passengers wait for the Herne Bay bus to take them home. The buildings of the Simon Langton boys' school are in the background.

A similar view from late 1960, a few months after the whole Langton complex, together with no. 13 St George's Lane, had been levelled. This freed up the site for the realignment and widening of the lane, as well as the construction of Riceman's.

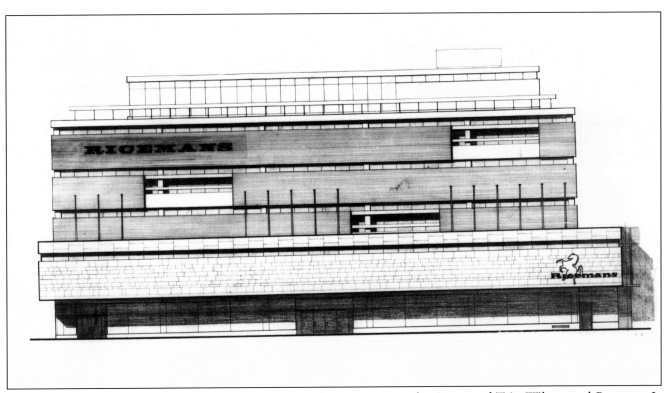

A drawing of the proposed Riceman's store. The architect was Sir John Burnet of Tait, Wilson and Partners. It would prove to be the first post-war building to defy the 'mediaeval scale' of Canterbury, thus far adhered to by the 1950s developments.

A 1961 view of the beginning of construction work for the massive new store. The 1950s colonnade of shops, on the south side of St George's Street, respectfully allows an almost unobstructed view of the cathedral that would soon be lost.

The steel and concrete frame of Riceman's begins to rise above the surrounding new developments, in this view from late 1961. The strip of land in the foreground would soon be utilised for the new St George's Lane dual-carriageway.

The frame of the new structure is complete, and cladding of the external elevation has now begun. The building contractors were, once again, Richard Costain Ltd. The 'topping off' ceremony would shortly take place, at the end of May 1962.

Mr Fred Riceman addresses a gathering of some 80 workmen in the basement of his nearly completed store, during May 1962. The 'beer and hamburger' party was a thank you to the workforce for the hard work they had, so far, put in to realise Fred's dream.

A gathering of the Riceman family, senior Riceman officials and directors from Costain's grouped on the roof of the new store, during the 'topping off' celebrations, at the end of May 1962. The group includes Fred's two sons, David and Jonathan.

A study of Fred Riceman, taken on the roof of his nearly finished building. With branches already in Deal, Herne Bay and Whitstable, the new store in Canterbury was the realisation of a seven year struggle to 'join his fortunes with those of the historic city'.

The all but completed Riceman's store, on 17 August 1962, exactly one month before opening. St George's Lane, closed at this point since the construction of the bus station in 1956, had yet to be laid along its new route, currently occupied by taxis.

Monday 17 September 1962 and rain dampens some of the 250 volunteers who took part in the 'Canterbury Through the Ages' procession that preceded the opening of the store. One soggy Viking looks up at the new building.

The inclement weather has not dampened the spirits of the crowds lining St George's Lane, as 'Henry II' does his penance, exactly as he had in 1174 shortly after the murder of Thomas Becket by the hands of his own knights.

'Henry II' is followed by a group of crusaders, two of whom are mounted. In total, 40 horses were used in the 'Canterbury Through the Ages' parade. The parade of shops behind were built in 1957 and demolished in 1999.

A smiling page 'boy' holds up a banner to announce the arrival of Geoffrey Chaucer and his bawdy pilgrims. The procession had begun at the Westgate and passed up the full length of the main street before ending in front of the new Riceman's store.

Members of the 'New Model Army' seem to be enjoying the occasion as the round head leader barks the command to halt in front of Riceman's. It is clear from this view that the reconstruction of St George's Lane had not been finished in time.

'Charles II' acknowledges the cheers of the people of Canterbury, recalling that the real thing had passed through the city in 1660, on his way to the restoration. A proud Mr Bill Dawson, who organised the procession, looks on (right).

Surrounded by members of his family, Mr Fred Riceman addresses the crowd, just prior to the store opening. He remarked that everyone had been so busy with the preparations that they had forgotten what it is like to have any time off.

Seventeen-year-old Miss Elizabeth Riceman, the youngest member of the family, cuts the satin ribbon following her declaration of the store's opening. She had been allowed the day off from Benenden School to officiate at the ceremony.

With the doors finally open, the crowds surge into the new building to join Mr Jonathan Riceman (bottom right). The takings on the first afternoon were satisfactory, considering that most people mainly came for a good look at the merchandise on display.

A gathering on the roof of Riceman's, following the opening ceremony. They are (left to right): Mrs Betty Riceman, the Mayor, the Revd Clive Pare, Fred, Mrs Pare and Elizabeth Riceman.

Flames leap from the top floor of the Riceman's store around about midnight on Saturday 23 March 1963, barely six months after the official opening. The fire broke out only 30 minutes after late-night diners and restaurant staff had left the building.

Spectators view the conflagration from the safety of the city wall opposite. The *Kentish Gazette* reported that hundreds of people gathered in the streets to watch and police reinforcements had to be called in to control the crowds.

Firemen clamber over charred smoking furniture and twisted steel girders of the Grace and Favour restaurant, where it is thought, the fire broke out. The skill of the fire brigade and the design of the building prevented the fire spreading to the rest of the store.

Mr Fred Riceman and the restaurant manager, Mr Norman Grace, examine the remains of the fifth floor shortly after the building was safe to enter. Inevitably, the remaining floors, although saved from the fire, suffered from water and smoke damage.

Work in progress to rebuild the top floor of Riceman's, in June 1963, as seen from the surface car park behind. The temporary buildings (bottom left) served as offices, including one for Fred Riceman, to replace those lost in the fire.

Disc jockey David Jacobs cuts the ribbon to officially re-open the rebuilt store, on Wednesday, 18 September 1963. Staff members behind include the head of advertising, Chris Gay (left) and Mr David Riceman (centre).

David Jacobs signs autographs in the mans shop, a process that took some 45 minutes. Each grateful recipient of a signature was asked to donate sixpence to the 'Helping Hands' charities.

The area immediately behind the Riceman store, in December 1969. Much of it, including that covered by most of Gravel Walk, was once occupied by the Simon Langton Schools. Note the surviving section of mediaeval wall marooned in the car park.

The beginning of the construction for the Whitefriars Shopping Centre, behind the existing Riceman's building, in June 1971. The scheme, opened in 1973, into which Riceman's extended, did not include the floor space they had originally requested.

Riceman's and the Whitefriars development, seen from the roof of Marks & Spencer, in 1988. By this time, Riceman's had not only added a second floor to the scheme (1974) but also taken over the floor space once occupied by International Stores (1982).

The Multi-storey Car Park

THE Wilson Development Plan (and later amendments under John Berbiers) very much planned the new post-war Canterbury around the needs of the motorist. Not only was there to be a complete ring road, but also a cross-city east to west relief road (of which Gravel Walk was to be part) and a secondary north to south relief road. Ultimately, there would also have been four multi-storey car parks. By the mid-1960s, the sites for the first two had been identified. One would be at Blackfriars, roughly where the Millers Arms pub is situated, the other at Whitefriars between Gravel Walk and Watling Street.

In 1964, the site chosen for the Whitefriars Multi-storey still contained a number of surviving pre-war buildings, especially along the south side of Gravel Walk. Here could be found two white rendered detached houses, one Regency, one Victorian. There was also the premises of Drew's Coaches, the buildings of Williams the coach builder and a small non-conformist burial ground. In Rose Lane, there was an old garage building that became famous in the film *A Canterbury Tale*, for it was here that the heroine of the film stored her caravan.

By the end of 1965, all the above mentioned buildings had been demolished. Only the burial ground remained, marooned in the middle of a new temporary surface car park and even that was to go before long. Mid-1960s plans for the multi-storey car park shows that the design, as built, had already been settled on, the major difference being that then, it was to be two storeys higher. Construction work began in 1968 and there was much civic excitement in what was perceived as a parking panacea. The structure was officially opened in 1969 by Lord Cornwallis, but was treated with caution by motorists who initially preferred the surface car parks.

Over the years, the multi-storey has attracted much negative publicity, being a focus for suicide attempts, as well as the drive off accidents. Its brutalist architectural style has also won it few friends. People's general attitude, with regards to bare concrete structures, seems to be to join the chorus of condemnation and write them off as mere 1960s 'carbuncles', without actually looking at them. The staircase towers of Canterbury's multi-storey were architecturally very dramatic, almost sculptural. The Gravel Walk elevation was less successful, although the maturing poplar trees and clinging ivy of recent years provided some green relief.

However, now it is gone and everyone will have to find another building to hate.

The recently cleared site of the Simon Langton Boys' School, as viewed from the St George's Street shops, in about 1961. Beyond, are Gravel Walk and the miscellany of sites and buildings then still to be found on the narrow lane's south side.

The junction of Gravel Walk and Rose Lane in August 1962. The chestnut paling fence (left) marks the line of the recently demolished Whitefriars perimeter wall (see chapter nine). Right, is the Regency period house at no. 7 Gravel Walk.

Another view of no. 7, on the south corner of Gravel Walk and Rose Lane, in March 1964. By this time, Gravel Walk had been vastly widened and the old course of the lane become a pavement. The old house was now occupied by the Ministry of Health.

The buildings immediately behind no. 7 Gravel Walk, on the Rose Lane frontage, in March 1964, once occupied by W.S. Williams & Son, Coachbuilders. The old brick garage (right) had featured in the 1943 film *A Canterbury Tale*.

Another view of the former coachbuilder's premises, and the famous old garage building, the top storey of which had been lost in the October 1942 blitz. In the film, the heroine, played by Sheila Sim, had kept her caravan stored here.

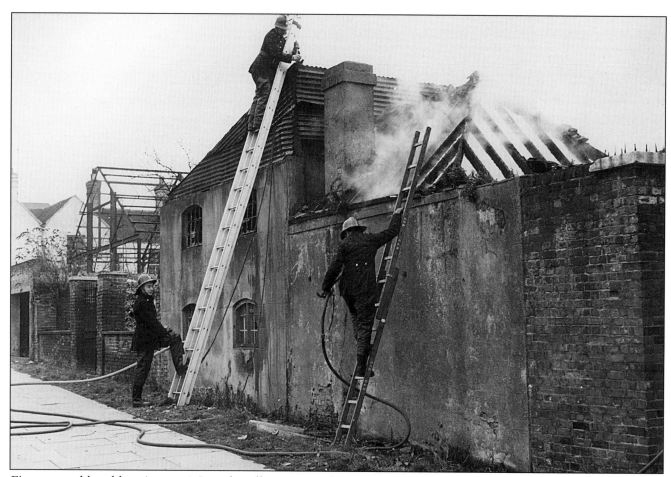

Firemen tackle a blaze in no. 6 Gravel Walk, on 1 April 1964. The building had recently been used by Williams & Son as a paint store. Further along the south side of Gravel Walk can be seen the premises of Drew's Coaches and a house at no. 3.

The brick pillars and iron gateway to a small burial ground that could be found halfway along the south side of Gravel Walk. It had been established towards the end of the 19th century, to serve both the nearby St Mary Bredin and Nonconformist church.

A view just inside the gates of the burial ground, dating from February 1963. The author's paternal grandfather recalled that some World War One German prisoner of war graves could be found herein. The Nissen huts (right) were part of Williams & Son premises.

The eastern edge of the burial ground with a miscellany of gravestones. Beyond the wall, is the skeletal garage building for Drew's Coaches who for many years, operated a service from the bus station to St Augustine's Hospital.

The rusty hulks of two ancient cars and one lorry languish in the long since blitzed premises of E.J. Philpot Ltd, at the top end of Gravel Walk (south side). Behind is the end wall of the white rendered house at no. 3 Gravel Walk.

An early 1960s view of the buildings between the top end of Gravel Walk and Watling Street, not as yet linked by St George's Lane. The single-storey industrial complex would shortly be demolished to make way for the proposed road extension.

A spring 1967 view of the junction of St George's Lane and Gravel Walk, both now widened, but the former, not yet extended through to Watling Street. Also by this time, all the old buildings between Watling Street and Gravel Walk had been pulled down.

A massing study for the proposed multi-storey car park, that is, an assessment of the new building's impact on the cityscape, as seen from the Riding Gate. Views of the cathedral had already been compromised by the bulk of the Riceman's store.

A City Council drawing of the new multi-storey car park, as unveiled to the public in October 1966. Designed by the City Architect, Mr Donald Tompkinson, the structure was initially intended to accommodate some seven floors of car parking space.

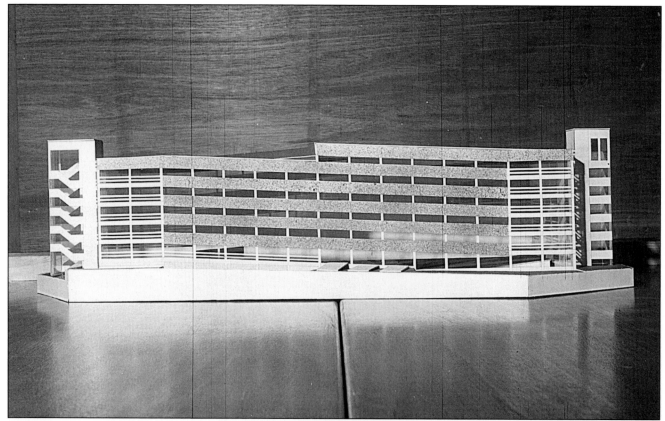

A model of the proposed multi-storey from March 1968, which by this time, had been reduced to six floors. The government and the Royal Fine Art Commission were not happy with the building's size and wanted views of the Cathedral preserved.

Tower cranes over White-friars indicate that construction work for the multi-storey car park had begun. This September 1968 view is from Watling Street. Further pressure from the government, meant that the city were now building a five-storey structure.

Members of the City Council Planning Committee being given a tour of the multi-storey construction site in December 1968. They are standing near what would become the structure's Watling Street entrance.

Former Mayor, Stanley Jennings, leads the council delegation across the multi-storey basement, during the December 1968 inspection. The building contractors were Truscon Ltd, who had also designed London's first multi-storey in 1934.

Concrete being delivered by tower crane to the multi-storey site, during the City Council's tour of inspection. This view is from Rose Lane, with Marlowe Motors to the right.

The much widened Gravel Walk, looking east in the spring of 1969, with construction work on the multi-storey car park progressing well. This view makes an interesting comparison to those at the beginning of this chapter.

Traffic queues in Watling Street in spring 1969, with the multi-storey construction clearly evident to the right. Also note the strip of land earmarked for the St George's Lane extension, currently serving as a temporary car park.

The Mayor, Councillor Herbert Buckworth (right), speaking at the opening ceremony for the multi-storey, on 7 November 1969. The official opening was carried out by Lord Cornwallis (centre), the Lord Lieutenant of Kent and Canterbury.

Lord Cornwallis speaking at the opening of the multi-storey, being watched by his wife, who had just been presented with a bouquet.

His lordship unveils the plaque, watched by the Mayor, Alderman Dalton and Mr E.A. Kirkby, managing director of contractors Truscon Ltd.

The invited guests at the opening ceremony on 7 November 1969, gathered round the multi-storey's Watling Street entrance. Lord Cornwallis remarked that use of the new car park would help people avoid the 'yellow perils' and resultant parking tickets.

The brutalist concrete staircase tower and façades, as seen from the newly extended St George's Lane, in January 1970. The contractor commented that it was difficult to fit a raw concrete structure into mediaeval backgrounds, but felt that it had been achieved.

The multi-storey car park from Gravel Walk in 1988, a view that will be familiar to most of us. By this time, Lombardy Poplars and climbing ivy had begun to soften the structure's uncompromising impact on the cityscape.

An inglorious end to a building, for which most people felt confident to express a dislike for, secure in the knowledge that few would disagree. This 12 September 2001 view from Gravel Walk, shows the structure now bisected by the demolition plant.

The 1970s

THE early 1970s started where the late 1960s left off as far as the Whitefriars area was concerned, in that the redevelopment of the area continued with large scale modernist buildings. In fact the early 1970s would see this process completed.

Much of the former Simon Langton area was still a surface car park and it was here that construction of the Whitefriars shopping arcade began in 1971. The new scheme provided much additional shop space including an extension for both Marks & Spencer and Riceman's.

The new scheme was linked to the multi-storey by means of an over bridge that also included a Morelli's Restaurant (completed in 1973) and connected to the main St George's Street thoroughfare by means of an escalator and small bridge over the service area. The scheme was completed by a small tower block for Midland Bank, which employed the same imaginative architectural style as the adjacent stair lobby for the arcade.

With the Whitefriars development completed, nothing much happened for the next 20 odd years. In the mid-1990s, Marks & Spencer added another floor on top of their part of the Whitefriars Arcade Scheme. Given the City Council's current obsession with past architectural styles, what resulted was the utterly bizarre spectacle of a modernist block with a series of tiled gables perched high on top of it.

At the time of writing, all of the architecture described above, with the exception of the Marks & Spencer extension has been destroyed, or is about to be demolished, for the current scheme.

A final trip into our study area and through the Riding Gate, which by October 1970, was about to be dismantled and replaced by a concrete over bridge. The city wall to the right was already being reconstructed in concrete, with a flint outer layer.

Workmen drill away the road metalling over the 87-year-old wrought iron bridge, to allow it to be cut into sections and lifted clear by crane. Note the large quantities of East Kent double-deckers, in the bus station, wearing the much missed red and cream livery.

An identical view, from February 1971, with the concrete span of the new bridge in place. It is the fifth known version of the Riding Gate, preceded by twin Roman arches, a mediaeval arch and bastion, a Georgian brick bridge and the Victorian iron bridge of 1883.

On-street parking in Rose Lane during December 1971. By this time, plans for the pedestrianisation of St George's Street were well advanced, a move that would greatly increase the traffic use of Rose Lane and banish on-street parking forever.

A traffic mishap in St George's Street during July 1970. A Ford Corsair from St George's Lane had collided with a bus from St George's Street. Perhaps the recent opening of St George's roundabout had confused either one or both of the drivers.

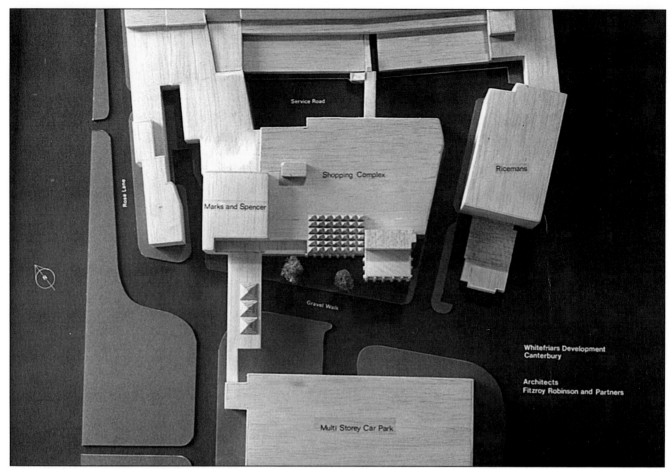

A model of the proposed Whitefriars Shopping Centre, on public display in June 1971. This, the last great modernist development in the city centre, would effectively complete the post-war rebuilding of Canterbury.

An architects drawing of the proposed bridge and café over Gravel Walk, that would link the multi-storey car park to the new shopping scheme.

Another depiction from June 1971, this one showing the planned bank tower in Gravel Walk and adjacent lobby to the shopping centre.

Contractors move on to the Whitefriars surface car park in January 1971, in preparation for the construction of the new shopping scheme. Centre view, a temporary loading bay is being constructed for Marks & Spencer.

March 1971 and preliminary work for the Whitefriars Shopping Centre had begun. This view from Riceman's shows the car park that for many years, had been the grounds of the Simon Langton Schools and before that, the precincts of a mediaeval friary.

Pile driving for the new shopping scheme, under way in March 1971. The pile is being driven into the area, near to where the last stretch of surviving mediaeval Whitefriars wall had recently been pulled down.

Subterranean foundations being laid for part of the shopping scheme, in June 1971. This would eventually be the site of the Midland Bank block and the Riceman's extension. During the construction, little or no archaeological work was carried out.

The temporary goods reception building for Marks & Spencer, in the service yard between the St George's Street colonnade (right) and the new shopping scheme (left), in 1972.

Construction work in progress for the Whitefriars Shopping Centre, in 1972, as seen from the Marks & Spencer loading area. The new scheme would eventually be linked to the main St George's Street thoroughfare by means of an escalator and over bridge.

The main supporting legs and girders for the combined over bridge and café building, being installed across Gravel Walk, in May 1972. This would allow users of the multi-storey to cross into the new shopping scheme in safety.

Gravel Walk in January 1973, with work well advanced on the new Midland Bank building. Further down is the, by now, completed café/over bridge and the new Marks & Spencer extension (right).

A January 1973 view, from the new over bridge, looking towards the Marks & Spencer extension building. The voids in the bridge sides would soon be filled with iron maps, showing the development phases of the city over the centuries.

The imposing Gravel Walk elevations of both the Midland Bank tower and stair lobby of the White-friars Shopping Centre (left), newly completed in September 1974. The interesting pyramid shaped light wells atop the lobby building can just be seen.

The new ground floor banking hall, viewed from the main entrance in Gravel Walk. The first floor comprising securities, foreign exchange and suite of managerial offices, could also be accessed directly from the first floor level of the new shopping scheme.

A reception at the opening of the new Midland Bank branch on 16 September 1974. In attendance with their wives were (left to right) : Mr P. Nicholson, regional director, branch manager Mr Dennis Le Sueur and general manager Mr L Needham.

The Destruction of Modernist Whitefriars

AS soon as plans for the 1990s Whitefriars redevelopment were submitted, it became clear that, with the exception of the Marks & Spencer extension, all the existing post-war buildings on the central Whitefriars site would be demolished. It was stated that they were redundant, ill suited to conversion and that their locations, surrounded as they were by broad roads and service areas, made the comprehensive redevelopment of the whole area the only choice. A council spokesman even stated publicly, that all the existing buildings had been hurriedly put up in the early post-war years, which was clearly not true.

One could argue that there were alternatives to comprehensive redevelopment or that some buildings of architectural merit be retained. However, such discussions were rendered academic in late 1999, when demolition began. The first buildings to go were the terraced shops on the east side of St George's Lane, the former Sun Building and the bus station offices. This was to allow for the re-alignment of St George's Lane and the relocation of the mains services away from the redevelopment area. In 2000, MacDonald's (the former Pricerite's) and the buildings on either side were demolished in advance of the 'Big Dig'. Also pulled down in the same year were the former Coach and Horses pub in St George's Lane and former Barrett's 1960 showroom building in Rose Lane.

2001 saw everything between Gravel Walk and Watling Street swept away. Watling House perished in March, but it was the destruction of the United Reformed Church in April that was hard to accept. Its clear position as one of Canterbury's finest early post-war buildings seemed to have been lost on the powers that be.

Having chipped away at the church's lobby and hall, the demolition gang finally flattened the main body of the church at night under floodlights, as if the act was too shameful to be witnessed.

The multi-storey car park was very publicly demolished from August to October. At the very end, for just two days, the eastern staircase tower stood alone. People who otherwise disliked the multi-storey and witnessed this last defiant fragment, agreed what a dramatic statement it made and even expressed a wish that it somehow be retained.

From late October onwards, the demolition contractors turned their attention to the early 1970s Whitefriars Shopping Arcade. At the time of writing, the last remains of the former Midland Bank tower were being taken down.

Having torn a huge chunk out of the former Sun Building, the demolition machine continues by further reducing the terrace of shops on the east side of St George's Lane. It is 24 November 1999 and the work is being carried out from the rear service yard.

The 1957 built row of shops on the east side of St George's Lane, as seen from the city wall, and across the rear service yard, in 1988.

The terrace of shops in St George's Lane being demolished on 18 November 1999. This was the first clearance to be carried out for the Whitefriars redevelopment scheme.

MacDonald's, the former Pricerite supermarket building of 1960, on the rounded corner between St George's Lane and St George's Street. The cityscape was familiar to many over many years.

The former burger house and supermarket now reduced to a mere curved curtain wall, as viewed from the rear service area on 6 July 2000.

The ominous sign of scaffolding being erected against the buildings at the top end of St George's Street on 20 May 2000, a sign that demolition is about to begin.

Exactly a month later, on 19 June 2000, their destruction is in progress. This view is captured from the fire escape for the 1970s Riceman's extension.

The three unregarded two-storey shops that bridge the gap between Riceman's and MacDonald's, on the west side of St George's Lane, built in the early 1960s.

Demolition, again viewed from the rear service area, taking place on 6 July 2000. The as yet, untouched Riceman's is on the far right.

The west side of St George's Lane, as seen from the Gravel Walk junction, in July 1997. The former Coach and Horses pub of 1963 is in the foreground.

The site of the pub on 28 January 2001, viewed from the eastern staircase tower of the multi-storey car park. The cellar walls are the only traces that remain.

A mid-1990s view of Watling House, completed in 1966, on the corner of Watling Street and Rose Lane. By this time, the former ground floor car showrooms had become a bazaar for discount clothes.

The rear of Watling House being reduced to a concrete skeleton during demolition work, on 22 March 2001. The multi-storey again provides the vantage point.

The United Reformed Church in its last days, as seen from the multi-storey, on 11 April 2001. By this time, work on the curious replacement church opposite was nearly complete.

The incredibly sad sight of the much loved church being demolished, on 19 April 2001. The main body of the church came down at night shortly afterwards.

A mid-1980s view of the Morelli's Café Shoppe, that also served as a bridge linking the multi-storey to the 1970s Whitefriars shopping scheme.

The over bridge being cut up for scrap on 5 September 2001. Behind, the multi-storey car park, no longer a convenient vantage point, is also passing into history.

The much hated multi-storey car park on a quiet Sunday morning in August 1997. Viewed through different more imaginative eyes, its brutalist shapes could become quite fascinating!

The eastern staircase tower standing alone on 9 October 2001, a fragment that took on an almost sculptural appearance for the few days before it too was toppled.

Whitefriars Unrealised

IT COULD be said that in Canterbury's recent history, no part of the city has been subject to so many unrealised plans or projects as the Whitefriars area. The nightmare of unfulfilled dreams began in the 1930s, when the then City Council conceived the idea of a new Civic Centre on the Dane John. This would be linked to the Cathedral by a grand Civic Way, effectively a processional roadway that would symbolically link the two main city buildings representing the church and state.

The redundant Dane John Brewery was demolished in the mid-1930s as a prelude, but World War Two put the whole scheme on hold. Ironically, the bombing of June 1942 and its uncompromising post-blitz clearance programme, provided the blank slate that made the revival of these plans possible.

Both Civic Centre and Civic Way were included in the 1945 Holden Development Plan, a controversial and comprehensive redevelopment of much of the entire city, both blitzed and unblitzed, that included the entire Whitefriars area. This plan required no less than 75 acres of compulsory purchase to realise. The private enterprise lobby opposed the plan and successfully put up candidates in the October 1945 local elections to defeat it. What resulted was the compromise that became the Wilson Plan of 1947, which got under way in 1951. Even this plan required 33 acres of compulsory purchase and once again, the entire Whitefriars area was included. The Wilson Plan and the concept of compulsory purchase, petered out in about 1953 as government funding dried up.

The 1960s promised a brighter future and new City Architect, John Berbiers, planned the wholesale redevelopment of the Whitefriars area as a modernist utopia. Again, a Civic Centre was included, to replace many of the Dane John's Regency buildings, but the Civic Way was replaced by a widened and staggered Rose Lane (a Civic Way in everything but name). Once again though, as with the 1950s, lack of central funding curtailed the more ambitious aspects of these plans. However, this time the implications were more serious in that Canterbury's status as a county borough was threatened by local government reorganisation. Without this, a Civic Centre could not be justified, nor would one be appropriate. Indeed, this is just what happened. John Berbiers left the city at the end of 1965, his more radical plans never to be realised.

It is interesting to note that the more ambitious plans of the 1950s and 1960s, were unrealised because they were too forward looking. Ironically, some of the late 1990s plans, for the comprehensive redevelopment of the Whitefriars area, were unrealised as they were too backward looking. Two of the four rival development plans submitted for public consultation, were largely based on vernacular pastiche, which although appealing to the man in the street, did not find favour with the local societies, lobby groups or Canterbury historians. On the other hand, equally out of favour was the brave submission by the British Design Partnership with its unashamedly modernist key buildings, linked by smaller scale post-modernist developments. Its sensitive yet exciting treatment of the Dane John end of the site, with neo-Regency houses by Anthony Swaine, coupled with an ultra-modernist United Reformed Church (that mirrored the shape of the Dane John Mound) will forever remain one of the Whitefriars area's most tantalising unrealised plans.

The City Surveyor, Mr Millson Enderby OBE, studies a model of the 1945 Holden Plan, the first and most radical redevelopment scheme for post-war Canterbury. Behind him, Hugh Wilson, John Boyle and John Barrett consider other documents.

A mid-1930s view of the route for the proposed Civic Way. In the foreground, is the site of the recently demolished Dane John Brewery. Other clearance work would have followed had not the war intervened and ironically provided the space needed.

A drawing of Holden's completed Civic Way (presented in 1945), looking towards the Cathedral from the proposed Civic Centre. It would completely replace Rose Lane.

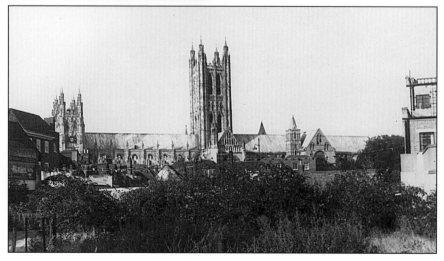

The reality: the blitzed and overgrown route of the Civic Way in the late 1940s. By then, Holden's plans were scrapped but the Civic Way was still on the drawing board.

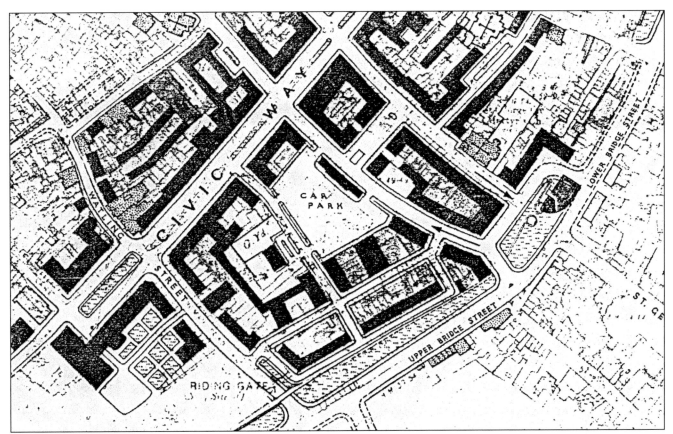

An extract from the planning map for the 1945 Holden Plan, showing its affect on the Whitefriars area. New buildings are shown in dark blocks. The Civic Way replaces Rose Lane and the east-west relief road cuts across the Langton site.

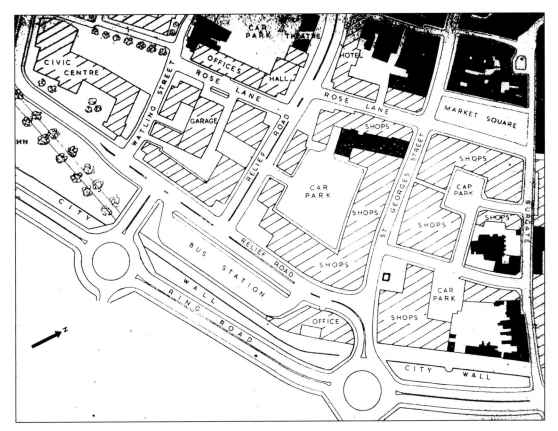

The Wilson Plan, first conceived in 1947 and presented to the public in 1951. This extract also shows the Whitefriars area, but with much that was actually carried out. The notable exception being the Civic Centre (top left).

An early 1960s model of the John Berbiers-designed Civic Centre, with the separate Council Suite building in front of the administrative block.

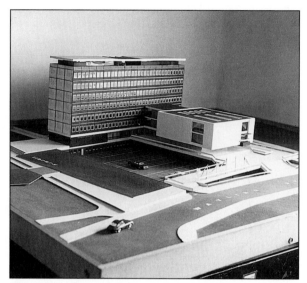

The revised model from May 1965, with a completely redesigned Council Suite building fronting Watling Street.

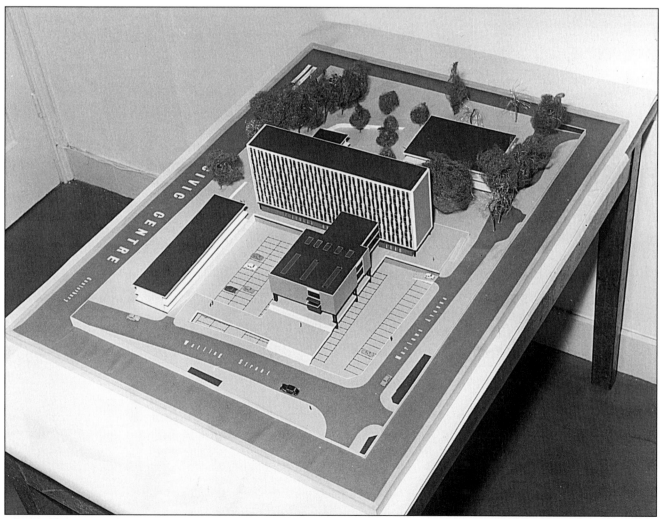

The final version of the proposed Civic Centre, from October 1965, this time with the administration block redesigned. Mr Berbiers was very excited about this version of the plan, especially the new façades to the larger block with its 'perpendicular influences'.

John Berbier's vision of the completed 1960s Whitefriars, with the Civic Centre in the foreground replacing all the Regency buildings in the Dane John. It is interesting to note the early design for the multi-storey car park (centre).

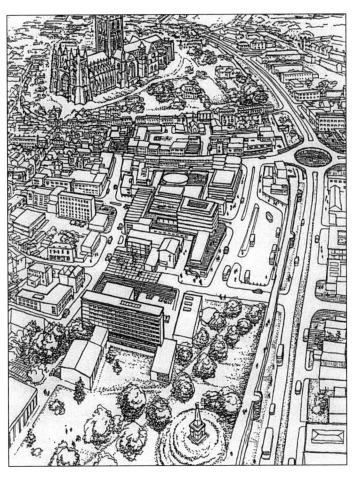

Mr John Berbiers in December 1956, having just replaced Hugh Wilson as City Architect; an unashamed modernist and a man much liked by all who worked with him.

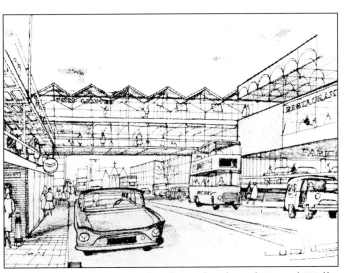

Berbier's 1965 concept for the redeveloped Gravel Walk, then destined to become part of a cross-city relief road. Compare this view to the realised one in chapter 16.

The proposal for the redevelopment of Watling Street, as conceived by the Building Design Partnership in 1996. They were one of the four architectural groups, chosen by the city council, whose rival designs would be submitted for public consultation.

Well known Canterbury based architect and Freeman of the City, Anthony Swaine, who as part of the Building Design Partnership, was responsible for the more sensitive Watling Street area (where the group's more modernist ideas were tempered).

An early submission by Chapman Taylor from June 1996, showing the St George's Lane proposals, as seen from the city wall. It is interesting to note how much these plans have changed and indeed improved, following their successful bid.

An overall view of the development proposals for the Whitefriars area as submitted by Renton, Howard, Wood, Levin in 1996. With the exception of one building in Watling Street, this design borrowed heavily on the architectural styles of the past.

The first of four rival designs for St George's Street, this one proposed by Building Design Partnership. Their mix of ultra-modernist and post-modernist buildings was very bold and ambitious, sadly perhaps, too much so for the stomachs of many citizens.

St George's Street as submitted by Lyons, Sleeman, Hoare, in June 1996. Note the 'Whitefriars Gate' building to the right. The group's plans, largely a pastiche of older styles, incorporated other 'gate' buildings including a rebuilt St George's Gate.

The 1996 Chapman Taylor proposals for St George's Street, showing a different design for their Riceman's (Fenwicks) replacement building, than was finally submitted. This drawing also shows the 1950s colonnade replaced rather than retained as now.

A 17th and 18th-century facsimile St George's Street, as submitted by Renton, Howard, Wood, Levin in 1996. Their plans included the retention of much of the 1950s colonnaded shops, but refaced to ape older buildings.

The proposals for Whitefriars Square by the Building Design Partnership. This new square would be at the junction of Gravel Walk and a new street, Whitefriars Street, running from St George's Street. Note the modernist library building design.

Whitefriars Square as submitted by Lyon, Sleeman, Hoare, could not be more different from the BDP, with its pastiche of older styles and the use of another 'gate' building, this one accessing the new library complex.